PERSUASIVE WRITING FOR LAWYERS AND THE LEGAL PROFESSION

Louis J. Sirico, Jr.

Professor, Villanova University School of Law

Nancy L. Schultz

Assistant Dean
George Washington University,
National Law Center

CONTEMPORARY CASEBOOK SERIES

Matthew Bender

Times Mirror
Books

1998 Reprint

Library of Congress Cataloging-in-Publication Data
Sirico, Louis J.
Persuasive writing for lawyers and the legal profession / Louis J. Sirico, Jr., Nancy L. Schultz.
p. cm. -- (Analysis and skills series)
ISBN 0-8205-2721-1
1. Legal composition. 2. Law--United States--Language. 3. Law--United States--Methodology. I. Schultz, Nancy L. II. Title. III. Series.
KF250.S54   1995   95-13054
808'.06634--dc20   CIP

MATTHEW BENDER & CO., INC.
EDITORIAL OFFICES
2 PARK AVENUE, NEW YORK, NY 10016-5675 (212) 448-2000
201 MISSION ST., SAN FRANCISCO, CA 94105-1831 (415) 908-3200

ACKNOWLEDGEMENTS

We would like to acknowledge the assistance and inspiration we constantly receive from our students. We wish to thank the students in the Advanced Legal Writing course at Villanova and the Advanced Oral Advocacy course at George Washington who have worked with some of the materials in this book. Louis Sirico would like to thank his colleague Diane Penneys Edelman. Nancy Schultz extends a special thank you to Christopher Colvin, Jay Davidson, Simon Nadler, John Pare, Todd Steinberg, and Julie Taub, whose work provided some of the models in this book. Nancy also wishes to acknowledge the continuing support and effort of Pam Chamberlain, who slogged her way through many drafts.

TABLE OF CONTENTS

Chapter 4

State Your Facts Persuasively

Chapter 5

Make Equity and Policy Arguments

Chapter 6

Use Precedent Persuasively

Chapter 7

Writing for Nonlegal Audiences

Chapter 8

Writing for Legal Audiences

INTRODUCTION

When new lawyers begin to practice their profession, they usually have acquired a sufficient knowledge of legal doctrine and at least a satisfactory proficiency at legal analysis. However, they often do not yet understand how to think and write like advocates.

Despite experiences like moot court, students spend most of their academic years objectively analyzing and evaluating court opinions and other legal documents. As a result, they can identify issues, explain the case law on both sides, and proffer at least a tentative conclusion. They also may prefer objective writing, because it entails less risk than advocacy: they do not have to take a position and defend it against assertive critics.

However, as many practitioners have told us, novice lawyers have difficulty switching from neutral writing to persuasive writing. For example, when writing an intra-office memo for a senior attorney, they may not be aware that they should be playing the advocate. They may be content with synthesizing and applying the relevant cases, statutes, and regulations. However, the senior attorney also wants to know if it is possible for his or her client to win. Therefore, novice lawyers also should be proposing ways to overcome the legal obstacles that they have identified.

Even when writing a brief, they may fail to write as assertively as they should. They also may not recognize that all sections of the brief, including the table of contents and statement of facts, are places for attractively portraying the client and its argument.

When beginning lawyers try to write like advocates, they sometimes misunderstand what persuasive writing is. They may think that learning persuasive writing requires learning a set of gimmicks—for, example, referring to your client by name and calling the other party by an abstract title like "the plaintiff" or "the appellee."[1] Although gimmicks may sometimes help—if the reader has not already seen them one time too many— they are not the key. Novice lawyers also may think that persuasive writing

---

[1] Rule 28(d) of the Federal Rules of Appellate Procedure requires you to be clear in identifying parties:

> Counsel will be expected in their briefs and oral arguments to keep to a minimum references to parties by such designations as "appellant" and "appellee." It promotes clarity to use the designations used in the lower court or in the agency proceedings, or the actual names of parties, or descriptive terms such as "the employee," "the injured person," "the taxpayer," "the ship," "the stevedore," etc.

requires them to adopt an overblown dramatic style. If so, they might have been more successful if they had lived in an earlier era. They also may think that persuasive writing requires ignoring strong arguments by opposing counsel and even ignoring adverse precedent. However, ignoring the opposition means giving up the opportunity to counter important arguments and sometimes even violates ethical rules.

In this book, we provide you with the keys to persuasive writing. They are not particularly dramatic. They consist of writing simply and clearly, consistently putting your best foot forward, while still arguing ethically and remembering to write for your audience.

By mastering these skills, you can stand out from your peers. Anyone who has read the briefs of practicing lawyers knows that too many are badly organized and barely comprehensible. Some skirt prohibitions by distorting critical facts and ignoring damaging precedent. You can easily produce a better work product.

If you organize your work product carefully and adopt a clear English style, you will have taken the most important steps to make your writing persuasive. If you also train yourself to structure your sentences, paragraphs, and documents in a way that encourages your reader to focus on your important arguments and react positively to them, you will become a consummate advocate.

For example, suppose that you represent the defendant, the Slope Corporation, a business in serious financial difficulty.[2] The plaintiff, Stanhope, Inc. issued Slope a letter of credit. On the basis of that letter, a bank is preparing to pay money to Slope. Stanhope argues that the letter of credit is invalid and seeks a preliminary injunction to stop the payment.

Slope and the bank argue that a preliminary injunction is extraordinary relief that is unnecessary here. According to their argument, Stanhope has readily available remedies at law that are less drastic than a preliminary injunction. They argue that Stanhope can pursue these remedies after the bank makes payment. If the letter of credit is valid and Slope fails to repay Stanhope, Stanhope can sue Slope. If the letter of credit is invalid, Stanhope can refuse to honor it.

In constructing your argument, you might write this paragraph:

Stanhope argues that it should be granted a preliminary injunction, because it will be difficult for it to recover a remedy at law. The fact of Slope's insolvency may pose an insuperable barrier to recovery, but Stanhope must be satisfied with a legal remedy. The adequacy of the remedy and not the possible lack of success in collecting it determine

---

[2] This example is based on 915 Company, Inc. v. Pennbank, 72 Erie (Pa.) County Legal J. 217 (1989).

whether a court should permit extreme interference with the defendant's conduct, that is, a preliminary injunction. So the case law holds.

Although this paragraph is grammatically correct and contains the pertinent information, it is far from being a compelling piece of advocacy. You could make the paragraph far more persuasive if you revised it this way:

> Because Stanhope has an adequate remedy at law, it cannot gain a preliminary injunction. As the case law holds, a court may grant a preliminary injunction when the legal remedy is inadequate and not when the plaintiff might have difficulty collecting it. Even if Stanhope finds Slope's insolvency a barrier to recovery, it cannot justify the extreme interference that a preliminary injunction entails. Stanhope must look to its remedy at law.

As you can see, you can improve your persuasiveness measurably by presenting your argument in an assertive way, reordering the presentation, and revising your sentences to make them more compelling. In this example, the three most effective techniques for improving persuasiveness are presenting information in an order that is easy to follow, using topic sentences, and ending the sentences in an assertive way.

In this book, we teach you how to write persuasively. A glance at the table of contents will give you a general idea of the lessons we present.[3]

We begin with a look at the big picture: making your arguments as simple as possible, adopting an assertive style, and organizing your writing. We then deal with paragraphs and sentences: structuring them to be persuasive, presenting facts skillfully, making equity and policy arguments, and using precedent to benefit your argument or at least not letting precedent injure it. Next, we discuss tailoring your argument to your audience. We then offer you a summary of the most important ethical rules governing advocacy. We conclude by introducing you to rhetorical flair by presenting a collection of paragraphs that employ classical rhetorical devices.

As you read the book, you will discover that the lessons are fairly simple and sometimes self-evident. These characteristics are evidence that they work. If the strategies were so subtle that you did not recognize them, you would know that they would not appeal to your common sense or to that of your audience.

The difficulty with learning persuasiveness lies in learning to apply the lessons and also in knowing when to reject them. To help you, we include a great number of examples with an emphasis on revising passages to make

---

[3] We base the structure of this book on Chapter 19 of Nancy L. Schultz, Louis J. Sirico, Jr. et al., Introduction to Legal Writing & Oral Advocacy (2d ed. Matthew Bender 1993).

them more persuasive. At the end of each chapter, we also offer exercises that permit you to work on developing your advocacy skills.

A word of caution is in order. Learning to write well is not a matter of learning rules and mechanically applying them. It is not about learning a formula; it is about learning an art. The lessons in this book will help you improve your writing only if you think about why they usually make writing more persuasive and then decide whether they will help improve your particular sentence, paragraph or document. In writing, creativity and reflection play a significant role.

Because good writing is an art, there is always room for improvement and room for disagreement. There are different ways to express the same idea effectively. For example, when you examine the many illustrations in this book, sometimes you will come across ways to make the good illustrations even more persuasive. By reflecting on the revisions that you would make, you will improve your understanding of the art of writing.

Before you begin studying these lessons on advocacy, you should give some thought to how you plan to internalize them. Although we have made an effort to limit the number of lessons, there are still quite a few, probably too many for you to make part of your writing style all at once.

Here are our suggestions. Begin by reading the chapters carefully. Working through the examples will give you experience in employing the relevant lesson. For more experience, complete the exercises at the end of each chapter. When you are drafting a brief or other major document, turn to the Table of Contents and use it as a checklist.

To improve your writing on a daily basis, pick the two or three lessons that you think will make the greatest improvement in your writing. Consciously apply them to your writing. When you start to apply them almost automatically, pick two or three more lessons and begin to apply them. Little by little, you can incorporate all the lessons into your writing style.

CHAPTER 1

MAKE YOUR ARGUMENT CLEAR AND CREDIBLE

[1] Make Your Argument as Simple as Possible

British political leader Lord Home once explained how he digested complex material: "When I have to read economic documents, I have to have a box of matches and start moving them into position to simplify and illustrate the points to myself."[1] Your goal is to present your arguments so simply that the reader does not need to carry around a box of matches and does not get the urge to use the matches for their usual purpose. The most important key to persuasive writing is to make your arguments as simple as possible.

If you make your critical arguments sound unnecessarily complicated, you can expect to hurt your case. The more difficult it is to understand your arguments, the more likely it is that the reader will give up or, even worse, reach a conclusion opposite from the one that you are advocating. You are more likely to persuade the reader with arguments that seem logical and simple and sound like common sense. Stick to your main arguments and write them so that they are easy to understand.

Here is a simple method for rooting out excessive complexity. Try to state your argument to a legal associate in a very few sentences. If he or she cannot follow your train of thought, revise your words and try again.

[a] Present Information in an Order That is Easy to Follow

The quest for simplicity begins with the sentence. Consider this example. In it, you are describing the actions of the trial court in a way that suggests that it was wrong.

> In summary, the trial court barred the defendants from explaining to the jury that their conduct was lawful according to their beliefs and barred them from substantiating the facts predicating those beliefs so as to show their beliefs to be reasonable by calling expert witnesses.

To understand the sentence's message, you probably had to read it more than once. Although the sentence is grammatically correct, it requires too much effort to comprehend. When you force a reader to piece together the meaning of an unnecessarily complicated sentence, you are not writing as persuasively as you could be.

---

[1] Oxford Dictionary of Modern Quotations 533 (Tony Augarde ed., 1991)

In this sentence, the argument sounds particularly complex, because the writer presents the information in a confusing order. In particular, the second half of the sentence requires surprising energy to understand and integrate into the meaning of the entire sentence.

We can make the sentence more digestible and more persuasive by reordering the way in which we present its content. If we wish to keep all the information in a single sentence, we can rewrite it this way:

> In summary, although the defendants believed that their conduct was lawful and had expert witnesses that could show that the beliefs were reasonable by substantiating the facts supporting those beliefs, the trial court barred them from explaining their beliefs to the jury and from calling the expert witnesses.

The underlying argument now seems simpler, because the sentence presents its message in an order that the reader can follow more easily. Although this version is easier to understand, it still requires excessive effort, because it contains too much information for a single sentence. We can simplify the argument more by using three sentences:

> In summary, the trial court refused to permit the jury to hear testimony showing that the defendants believed their conduct to be lawful and that this belief was reasonable. It barred the defendants from explaining to the jury why they believed they acted lawfully. In addition, it barred expert witnesses from substantiating the facts supporting the defendants' beliefs and thus from showing that their beliefs were reasonable.

We can improve comprehensibility even more by adding some verbal signals:

> In summary, the trial court refused to permit the jury to hear testimony showing, first, that the defendants believed their conduct to be lawful and, second, that this belief was reasonable. First, it barred the defendants from explaining to the jury why they believed they acted lawfully. Second, it barred expert witnesses from substantiating the facts supporting the defendants' beliefs and from thus showing that their beliefs were reasonable.

By including the words "first" and "second" as verbal signals, we give the reader a clear idea of the structure of our argument. This version contains the same information as the original. However, because we have simplified the structure of the presentation, the reader will find it more understandable and more persuasive.

[b] Focus on Your Main Arguments

When you write a law school exam, you expect to get credit for identifying and discussing the critical issues. You also expect extra points for discussing issues that are barely arguable or exceptionally complicated, even though they would be extremely artificial if raised in a "real world" legal argument.

The real world has a different system of grading. When you include numerous, complicated, artificial arguments in a legal brief or other persuasive document, do not expect the rewards that you garnered in law school. These arguments will distract the reader from the arguments with real persuasive power. They also may detract from your credibility. Stick to the arguments that have the best chance of winning. Heed the words of Judge Aldisert of the United States Court of Appeals for the Third Circuit:

> With a decade and a half of federal appellate court experience behind me, I can say that even when we reverse a trial court it is rare that a brief successfully demonstrates that the trial court committed more than one or two errors. I have said in open court that when I read an appellant's brief that contains ten or twelve points, a presumption arises that there is no merit to *any* of them.[2]

Deciding on what to focus is not always easy. Deciding to abandon or greatly deemphasize certain arguments is also difficult. However, these decisions may be the critical creative act that brings you success. The painter Hans Hoffman has written: "Every creative act requires elimination and simplification. Simplification results from a realization of what is essential."

We can illustrate this principle with an example from the briefs filed with the Supreme Court in *Stump v. Sparkman,* 435 U.S. 349 (1978). In that case, a mother filed a petition with Judge Harold Stump of the Indiana Circuit Court for authority to have her "somewhat retarded" daughter sterilized. Judge Stump signed the petition and the daughter was sterilized. A few years later, she learned what had happened and brought a civil rights action against several individuals, including Judge Stump. The issue before the Supreme Court is whether Judge Stump enjoys judicial immunity from the legal action. The Court ultimately found for Judge Stump.

Here are the headings and subheadings from the brief supporting Judge Stump:

    I.   The DeKalb County Circuit Court of which Harold D. Stump is presiding judge was at all times pertinent to this litigation a court of original, exclusive, general jurisdiction over all causes, matters and proceedings except those expressly removed from it.

---

[2] United States v. Hart, 693 F.2d 286, 287 n.1 (3d Cir. 1982) (emphasis in original).

II.   The doctrine of judicial immunity protects a judge from civil liability for any act within his jurisdiction done in the exercise of his judicial function.

III.   A court of general jurisdiction possesses the power of determining its own jurisdiction.

IV.   Judicial immunity is not lost through procedural errors, irregularities or deficiencies of a circuit court judge's acts. An "approval" is not an "order."

V.   At all pertinent times, Judge Stump acted in his judicial capacity. Judicial immunity exists for any act done by a judge in the exercise of his "judicial function."

VI.   In applying the doctrine of judicial immunity, the terms "jurisdiction" and "judicial function" are given broad definition.

VII. Only clear absence of all jurisdiction over the subject matter and that fact known to the judge will bring about a denial of immunity.

VIII. The opinion of the court of appeals is erroneous because it ignores, conflicts with and represents an unwarranted departure from the statutory authorities of the state of Indiana and the precedent of this court.

When you see an argument like this one with eight major headings, you dread having to read it. You know that the analysis will be complicated and probably badly organized. When you discover that the individual headings suggest a poorly structured argument and poorly structured sub-arguments, you know that reading the brief is going to be a struggle. Although you suspect that the kernel of a significant argument is buried in there somewhere, you do not know where to begin looking for it. You are not in a mood to be persuaded.

Could you reduce this diffuse argument to one with two or three major headings and a limited number of subheadings? Of course. Consider this revised version:

As the presiding judge in a court of general jurisdiction, Judge Stump is immune from civil liability for any act within his jurisdiction done in the exercise of his judicial function.

I. Judge Stump acted within the jurisdiction of the DeKalb County Circuit Court.

   A. As a court of general jurisdiction, the DeKalb County Circuit Court determines its own jurisdiction, and, here, Judge Stump decided that he had jurisdiction.

    B. Even if a judicial action contains procedural errors, irregularities or deficiencies, a court does not lose jurisdiction and a judge like Judge Stump retains judicial immunity.

    C. Judge Stump would lack immunity only if jurisdiction over the subject matter were clearly absent and the judge knew it, plainly not the case here.

II. Judge Stump acted in his judicial capacity and thus within the exercise of his judicial function.

    A. Judge Stump acted within his judicial capacity.

    B. For purposes of judicial immunity, the term "judicial function," like "jurisdiction," is defined broadly.

As you can see, this revision permits you to focus on the main points, which are in the introductory heading and two major headings. If you need a more detailed analysis, you can look to the subheadings.

Most of the argument in the original appears in the revision. The omitted arguments were either not compelling or distracted the reader from the main arguments. For example, although Headings VII and VIII in the original may be correct and may even have a place in the body of the argument, they do not warrant headings in the outline.

For purposes of comparison, consider the headings for the opposing brief arguing that Judge Stump is liable:

I. A judge is immune from civil liability only as to those judicial acts performed in exercise of his jurisdiction.

II. In the total absence of any judicial proceeding having been invoked or even contemplated, Judge Stump's secret approval of the permanent sterilization must be deemed a non-judicial act as to which no judicial immunity attaches.

Although we might wish for some subheadings to further delineate the analysis, these headings enable us to understand the argument. When we confront a brief that states its argument simply, we find it attractive and are likely to find it more persuasive than its counterpart with eight headings.

[c] Explain Technical Information

In today's world, the lawyer often must master the technology and vocabulary of such disciplines as engineering, medicine, economics, and the various sciences. Presenting technical arguments to a legal or lay audience is where the challenge lies. If you fail to provide a satisfactory explanation of technical terms and concepts, your audience may decide that your argument is just too complicated to grasp. To be an effective advocate, you must persuade your audience that it can understand your argument.

When you must use a technical word or phrase, define it first. Use as simple a definition as the circumstances permit. Include only those complexities that the reader must know to understand your argument and make a decision.

For example, suppose you are writing a brief that deals with waste from a nuclear power plant and requires you to refer to transuranic waste. You could define it as waste contaminated with alpha-emitting radionuclides of atomic number greater than 92 and half-lives greater than 20 years in concentrations greater than 100 nanocuries per gram. However, the judges may not need to have this level of understanding about transuranic waste. If not, your technical definition might put them in the wrong frame of mind to follow your argument. It might make them insecure about their ability to grasp your argument. It also might require them to spend so much time understanding the technicalities that they fail to follow the thrust of your argument.

To avoid the problem, you might define transuranic waste as waste that is not high-level waste but that still remains toxic for hundreds of years and requires long term isolation. If you believe that it is advisable to include the technical definition, you might place it in a footnote and place the simple explanation in the text.

In explaining complicated material, you may find it helpful to use analogies. An excellent illustration appears in *Carolina Environmental Study Group v. United States.*[3] There, Judge McMillan explains how a nuclear reaction takes place in a nuclear power plant:

> The fuel rods in the reactor stand on end, with vacant spaces among them.
>
> Control rods, with some type of insulation or shielding function, are let down from above and occupy the spaces among the fuel rods and separate the fuel rods, thereby preventing atomic reaction. The physical layout is roughly similar to that which would obtain if one hair brush were laid on a table with its bristles (fuel rods) sticking up, and another hair brush were pressed down on it with its bristles (control rods) pointing down.
>
> When heat is desired, the control rods are lifted, the fuel in the fuel rods starts reacting, and atomic fission or atom-splitting takes place.[4]

Judge McMillan begins by defining two technical terms, fuel rods and control rods, and then explains how a reaction takes place by making an analogy that uses a common item, a hairbrush.

---

[3] 431 F. Supp. 203 (W.D.N.C. 1977), rev'd sub nom. Duke Power Co. v. Carolina Envtl. Study Group, 438 U.S. 59 (1978).
[4] Id. at 206-07.

As you might guess, Judge McMillan's first career was as a trial lawyer. During the years spent persuading juries, he learned to explain complex material in simple terms. When he became a judge, he had to persuade members of the bench and bar that he had made correct decisions. His skills as a trial lawyer continued to come in handy.

[2] Write in a Persuasive but Credible Style

Some lawyers try to be persuasive by overstating their cases and by using emotionally charged verbs, adjectives, and adverbs. However, writing with a purple pen inevitably marks the practitioner as an amateur. Other lawyers state their cases without adding a persuasive edge of any sort. Their style does the client a disservice. It is possible to put your best foot forward without stepping over the line into obvious exaggeration.

For our generation of lawyers at least, there is a preferred style. It is assertive, but reasoned and even a little understated. This approach respects the intelligence of the audience. It allows the reader to be persuaded to adopt the writer's conclusion rather than attempting to force the conclusion on the reader in a way that might cause the reader to become defensive and reach a contrary conclusion. Consider this excerpt from a brief:

> Grantly's claim of false imprisonment shows complete ignorance of elementary tort law. The railroad is not liable, because it had more than ample grounds to detain him. Grantly's conduct was so outrageous that it demanded action by the railroad. Not only did he curse the female security officer and the ticket officer, but he went further. When asked to leave, he engaged in unwarranted abusive behavior by starting a shoving match with the male security officer.

Compare it with this version:

> Grantly's claim of false imprisonment fails, because he gave the railroad ample grounds to justify detaining him. He cursed the female security officer and the ticket agent and, when asked to leave, started a shoving match with the male security officer.

The first version gives no more information than the second. The overwriting distracts the reader from the core argument and probably irritates the reader who has heard this sort of rhetoric too many times to be persuaded by it. Moreover, the first sentence unnecessarily alienates the opposing lawyer.

Here, the facts are what persuade. If you want to make your argument more persuasive, add more relevant facts. You might quote or paraphrase Grantly's offensive language. If the male security officer suffered any injuries, you might describe them. If these events went on over a few minutes, you might state the duration to indicate the seriousness of the disturbance. The key is to persuade not with purple prose, but with facts and arguments.

To be clear, we are not recommending that you never use a pejorative adjective. For example, these sentences would be perfectly acceptable:

> Grantly was loud, abusive, and disorderly. His behavior gave the railroad the right to detain him.

The adjectives offer a telling summary. They are not used as a substitute for facts or as an attempt to intensify the impact of a sentence that should focus on facts. Instead, they serve a legitimate persuasive purpose.

Here is another example. Your client is suing the railroad, because it failed to repair a bridge. Whenever it rained, the bridge leaked, and a puddle or ice patch formed on the road below. Your client drove under the bridge, hit an ice patch, and lost control of her car. You argue that the railroad had notice of the problem. Here is a written argument that makes the point by relying on facts:

> The railroad had actual or constructive notice of this problem in at least two ways. First, it should have known that the spot was frequently the scene of accidents. Second, it had an engineering report giving notice of the bridge's condition.

If you wished to strengthen the argument, you would bolster it with facts. You might enumerate the number of reported accidents that occurred. You also might quote or refer to the critical language in the engineering reports. Your rewrite might read this way:

> The railroad had actual or constructive notice of this problem in at least two ways. First, it knew or should have known that the spot was frequently the scene of accidents—three serious accidents in the preceding five months. Second it had an engineering report executed for it that placed the bridge on a list of bridges needing maintenance or repair.

Here is an overwritten version of the same argument. As you read it you should recognize that the rhetoric fails to make the argument stronger and, by its distracting nature, probably weakens it.

> The railroad showed callous disregard for the public, because it had clear and unmistakable notice of this serious problem in at least two ways. First, the railroad would know that the spot was the scene of many tragic accidents. For it to deny such knowledge is inconceivable. Second, the railroad had in its possession its own internal engineering report that clearly reported the bridge's life-threatening condition.

An effort to avoid purple prose might lead some writers to underwrite and fill their sentences with unnecessary qualifiers. Here is an example:

The plaintiff claims that the railroad should have had notice of the problem. There are two ways in which the railroad might have known. First, the fact that the spot was frequently the scene of accidents—for some of which the spot may have been a contributing factor—is knowledge that a competently-run railroad or its supervisory administrators should have had. Second, the railroad had engineering reports executed for it indicating that the bridge was on a list of bridges in need of maintenance or repair.

This is not the prose of an advocate. If you did not know that this version was the product of the client's attorney, you would not guess it. This version has too many tentative verbs: "The plaintiff claims that"; "the railroad might have known"; and "the spot may have been a contributing factor." In addition, the part of the sentence beginning with "indicating" could be made stronger by using more concrete language: "placing the bridge on a list of bridges needing maintenance or repair."

The goal is to argue honestly, but still to put your best foot forward. The second version above meets these goals quite well. In contrast, the underwritten version bends over backwards not to overstate the client's case, and, therefore, does not advance it.

The rule about overwriting also applies to the way in which you characterize opposing counsel. Consider this paragraph from a court opinion:

> The English language, blending and building upon the vocabulary of its Latin and Germanic roots, is a marvelous and omnificient language, offering a rich variety of words and expressions to describe or explain a single thought. And so, in characterizing the complaint made in this appeal by Mr. David Bruce Baker, we have much to choose from—ludicrous, preposterous, silly, asinine, ridiculous, absurd, nonsensical, frivolous, outrageous, unreasonable, laughable, foolish, unsound, and incongruous come to mind, but there may be others. Meritless and erroneous are partly descriptive, but somehow they don't seem to capture the full flavor of the thought. In other words, we propose to affirm.[5]

Although a judge may be able to use this language to characterize an attorney's work—we have reservations—as an attorney, you should not. When you use such insulting words, you mark yourself as a bush-league lawyer.

You also may pay a price in the future. The next time you face the attorney that you have ridiculed, you may have a weak case and desperately want to settle. However, your opponent may be delighted to have the

---

[5] Marquardt v. Papenfuse, 610 A.2d 325, 327 (Md. Ct. Spec. App. 1992).

opportunity to repay your earlier compliments. In the end, your reputation and your client's case will suffer the repercussions.

[3] Deal with Contrary Arguments in an Affirmative Way

Some lawyers unwittingly put themselves on the defensive in the way in which they address the arguments of their opponents. Suppose you must refute the argument that a contract provision is unconscionable. Here is the wrong way to start out:

> Appellant incorrectly contends that the contractual provision limiting damages is invalid, because it is unconscionable. Contrary to its argument, the doctrine of unconscionability does not apply to these litigants who had equal bargaining power. Appellant's argument is not consistent with the case law.

In this paragraph, you begin by putting the opponent's argument first in a clear, succinct way. Then you state that the argument is wrong and begin to explain why.

The writing style is defensive. To be sure, you must deal with contrary arguments. To ignore them would be suicidal. However, you need not deal with them in a way that gives the reader the impression that the opponent is the assertive party. When you write this way, the reader may conclude that you are too overwhelmed by the opponent's arguments to formulate an affirmative argument of your own.

Here is a better way to address an opposing argument:

> The contractual provision limiting damages is valid. Because the litigants had equal bargaining power, the doctrine of unconscionability does not apply. Requiring unequal bargaining power as a prerequisite to unconscionability is a staple of the case law.

Here, we begin with an affirmative statement of our client's argument. Only then do we discuss the opponent's argument. Moreover, we deal with the issue in a way that emphasizes our affirmative argument: the contract is valid.

In this example, we do not directly state that the opponent has raised the issue of unconscionability. If we found it necessary to acknowledge that the opponent has made this argument, we would do so without overemphasizing the fact. We could revise the second sentence this way: "The litigants had equal bargaining power. Therefore, contrary to the opponent's contention, the doctrine of unconscionability does not apply."

Suppose that your client won in the trial court and now is defending that victory on appeal. You can make a particularly persuasive argument:

> As the trial court held, the contractual provision limiting damages is valid. Ruling against the appellant, that court correctly recognized

that the litigants had equal bargaining power and therefore the doctrine of unconscionability did not apply. The court's position follows the case law.

With a lower court's decision in your client's favor, you can strengthen your argument by invoking that authority. If your client loses in an intermediate appellate court, you still could stress your victory at the trial level. If you had a supportive dissent written by a respected jurist, you would note it. If you have neither a favorable decision below nor a persuasive dissent, you might emphasize a similar favorable case in another jurisdiction. We will discuss dealing with adverse authority again in Chapter 6.

EXERCISES

1. Mary Lufton is suing United Motors for injuries that she suffered in an automobile accident. She was driving a car manufactured by United Motors and claims that a design defect caused the accident. Since the accident, United Motors has made a change in its design. Lufton seeks to introduce the design change as evidence that her car was defectively designed. United Motors objects, invoking the state's evidentiary Rules 403 and 407.

Rule 403 states:

> Although relevant, evidence may be excluded if its probative value is substantially outweighed by the danger of unfair prejudice, confusion of the issues, or misleading the jury, or by considerations of undue delay, waste of time, or needless presentation of cumulative evidence.

In pertinent part, Rule 407 states:

> Whenever, after an event, measures are taken which, if taken previously, would have made the event less likely to occur, evidence of the subsequent measures is not admissible to prove negligence or culpable conduct.

In its memorandum to the court, United Motors outlines the argument this way:

I. Because the plaintiff alleges culpable conduct, Rule 407 applies to this action in strict liability.

II. Because the plaintiff alleges culpable conduct, Rule 407 excludes evidence of the design change.

III. To succeed in this strict liability action, the plaintiff must prove that United Motors engaged in culpable conduct.

IV. Therefore, plaintiff alleges culpable conduct by United Motors.

VI.   Therefore, Rule 407 excludes plaintiff's evidence of subsequent design change.

VII.   As a policy matter, excluding evidence of remedial measures encourages manufacturers to produce safer products.

VIII. As a policy matter, excluding evidence of remedial measures prevents the jury from incorrectly finding an admission of fault.

IX.   Because the probative value of evidence of the design change is substantially outweighed by the danger of prejudicing the jury, Rule 403 bars this evidence.

Please revise this outline so that it presents the argument in a simple form that is easy to understand.

2. In the same case, Mary Lufton outlines her argument this way:

I.   Because the plaintiff, Mary Lufton, does not allege culpable conduct, the evidence that United Motors took remedial measures is admissible

II.   Because Rule 407 does not apply to this action in strict liability, the evidence that United Motors took remedial measures is admissible.

III.   Because Lufton brings this action in strict liability, she is not alleging culpable conduct by United Motors.

IV.   Although Lufton could have brought this action in negligence, she has brought it in strict liability.

V.   Guided by proper instructions, the jury should be permitted to make an informed decision by fairly weighing all the relevant evidence.

VI.   Whether or not the evidence is admitted, a manufacturer is motivated to take remedial steps to avoid the risks of more legal actions and bad publicity.

VII.   Admitting evidence of remedial measures thus is supported by strong social policies.

VIII. Because the probative value of the evidence substantially outweighs the risk of prejudicing the jury, Rule 403 permits the jury to hear this evidence.

Please revise this outline so that it presents the argument in a simple form that is easy to understand.

3. Please revise this sentence to create one or more sentences that make your argument logical and easy to understand.

United Motors should not be granted a new trial where evidence of its subsequent design change would be excluded, because the trial court did not cause substantial prejudice to United Motors by admitting evidence of a subsequent design change.

4. You are describing to an educated, but nonscientific, audience the danger posed to the ozone layer in the stratosphere. You want to give your audience a general understanding of the role that industrial chemicals play in depleting the ozone layer. Here is a draft paragraph of your presentation. Please revise it so that it is not unnecessarily technical.

Human activity that depletes the ozone layer includes the use of industrial chemicals, most notably halocarbons and chlorofluorocarbons [CFCs]. The chemicals rise into the stratosphere where the sun's radiation breaks them down and causes them to release atoms of chlorine and bromine. These atoms react with the ozone molecules and destroy them. More specifically, the chlorine atoms attract ozone's third oxygen atom, and the ozone molecule decomposes into an oxygen molecule and a chlorine radical. When a chlorine monoxide molecule confronts a free oxygen atom, they form a new oxygen molecule and a chlorine radical. A free chlorine atom catalyzes numerous reactions that destroy more ozone molecules. Like chlorine, bromine atoms also destroy the ozone.

5. You represent Madeline Neroni, the plaintiff in a personal injury accident. While crossing at the intersection of two streets, Neroni was hit by a car that the defendant, Thomas Towers, was driving. Instead of crossing at the crosswalk, Neroni entered the street by passing between two cars parked south of the crosswalk. Towers argues that he is not liable, because Neroni assumed the risk. According to Towers, when Neroni exposed herself to danger by stepping out behind two parked cars, she fully appreciated the risk and exposed herself to it.

Here is a paragraph that you might include in your argument:

Towers argues that he is not liable, because Neroni assumed the risk. According to Towers, assumption of the risk arises here, because Neroni knew and appreciated the risk. However, even if the danger was obvious or discoverable by the exercise of reasonable care, a plaintiff who appreciates the danger does not assume the risk unless the plaintiff appreciates it fully. A full appreciation is not present here. If Neroni's conduct shows that she failed to appreciate the danger fully, she is, at best, contributorily negligent. Neroni's conduct falls short of assumption of the risk.

Please rewrite the paragraph so that is sounds less defensive and more affirmative.

CHAPTER 2

WRITE A WELL ORGANIZED ARGUMENT

The hallmark of many an unpersuasive argument is poor organization. A badly structured brief or report is a tremendous imposition on the reader. The reader must expend so much energy determining the organization of the argument that he or she has no energy with which to consider the argument itself. In addition, the reader may not know which arguments the writer is stressing.

The lesson is clear: Do not waste the reader's energy. To be persuasive, make the argument's organization easy to understand and encourage the reader to focus on the important points.

[1] Structure Your Argument

[a] Make Your Organization Readily Apparent

An important key to persuasive writing is producing a well organized document with a structure that the reader can follow easily. An obvious structure permits the reader to understand your argument as effortlessly as possible. Pass up stream-of- consciousness writing in favor of organization.

The way to organize is to write according to an outline and to put your conclusions first. Although legal education allegedly teaches students to "think like an outline," you still may not be the type of writer who is comfortable outlining before you write. In that case, write first and then reorganize so that your written product fits an outline. That is, write the outline after you have finished and then, where necessary, reorganize according to the outline.

Here is an example. Suppose that the government wins a conviction against the defendant for possessing cocaine, and now the defendant moves for a new trial in the interests of justice. The defendant argues that he received an unfair trial, because the court admitted as evidence a package of cocaine. According to the defendant, the police's chain of custody arguably had discrepancies. At various times, different officers were in charge of the evidence, and, in their reports, they described it slightly differently.

You are the government's attorney. In drafting a response, you might begin by writing a summary of the argument. It might look like this:

The evidence meets the "reasonable probability" test for admitting physical evidence, because a reasonable probability exists that the article has not been changed in important respects. There was no evidence of tampering; the procedures followed in handling the cocaine have been found adequate in the past. Additional evidence on the chain of custody would have been cumulative at best. The defendant's argument that further testimony might raise and answer questions is only conjectural. Three different police officers testified that the evidence was recovered from the defendant. Any discrepancies in the officer's testimony are insignificant, as the jury reasonably concluded. Moreover, at trial, the defendant had ample opportunity to bring out any inconsistencies in the testimony.

Your next step is to use this summary to write an outline of the argument. A natural part of devising the outline is to restructure the argument to make it clear and compelling. You must decide what arguments and information to emphasize and in what order to place them. In making these decisions, you should recall one of the lessons in Chapter 1: Make your argument as simple as possible.

You might begin by drafting a sentence that states your thesis and then decide on your major headings. After some thought, you might decide on this thesis sentence and two major headings:

The evidence meets the test for admissibility, because a reasonable probability exists that it was not changed while in custody.

    I.   The test for admitting physical evidence is that, in reasonable probability, the article has not been changed in important respects.

    II.   The evidence here meets the reasonable probability test.

You then would decide on subheadings. Your final outline might look like this:

The evidence meets the test for admissibility, because a reasonable probability exists that it was not changed while in custody.

    I.   The test for admitting physical evidence is that, in reasonable probability, the article has not been changed in important respects.

    II.   The evidence here meets the reasonable probability test.

      A.   Three different police officers testified that the evidence was recovered from the defendant.

      B.   There is no evidence of tampering: in the past, the procedures followed in handling the cocaine have been found adequate.

      C.   Additional evidence on the chain of custody would be cumulative at best.

1. It would be purely speculative to argue that further testimony might raise and answer questions.

2. At trial, the defendant had ample opportunity to bring out any consistencies in the testimony.

3. As the jury reasonably concluded, any discrepancies in the officers' testimony are insignificant.

If you follow this outline and make most of the headings topic sentences for your paragraphs, the structure of your argument will be readily apparent and persuasive. To illustrate the effectiveness of outlining, let us use the outline to construct a summary of the argument. It would look like this:

The evidence meets the test for admissibility, because a reasonable probability exists that it was not changed while in custody. The test for admitting physical evidence is that, in reasonable probability, the article has not been changed in important respects. Here, the package of cocaine was not changed in important respects.

The package of cocaine meets the reasonable probability test for two reasons. First, three different police officers testified that the evidence was recovered from the defendant. Second, there is no evidence of tampering. In handling the cocaine, the officers used procedures that have been found adequate in the past.

At the trial, sufficient evidence existed to establish the chain of custody; any new evidence would be cumulative at best. Therefore, a new trial to seek new evidence is unnecessary. It would be purely speculative to argue that further testimony might raise and answer questions. At the trial, the defendant had ample opportunity to bring out any inconsistencies in the testimony. As the jury reasonably concluded, any discrepancies in the officers' testimony are insignificant.

By comparing this summary with the initial version, we can see the difference that outlining makes. Although the initial version makes the same arguments, it requires the reader to engage in some effort to fully piece them together. In contrast, the revised version flows easily and, therefore, is more persuasive.

[b] State Your Argument at the End of the Introductory Paragraph

As we discuss later in this chapter, you usually will begin a paragraph with a topic sentence in which you state the paragraph's major idea. However, when you are beginning a document or a large section of a document, you normally should state your argument in a topic sentence at the end of the introductory paragraph or paragraphs. With this technique, you begin the paragraph by laying some groundwork for your argument and then build to a conclusion. In this way, you give some context for your argument and then let the reader know exactly what the argument is before he or she faces the task of digesting it in full.

To be an effective advocate, you need to place yourself in the shoes of your reader. The best way to start is to remember your experiences as a reader. Think of the times that you have read briefs, reports, or court opinions that did not state the argument or conclusion until the end of the document. You undoubtedly did not enjoy the suspense. In an effort to discover the conclusion, you probably peeked ahead. As a reader, you wanted to know right away where the argument was going. Your reader will have the same need-to-know that you had.

Here is an example. You represent the plaintiff in litigation over the title to real property. You lost at trial, because the court required you to prove your case by clear and convincing evidence and you could not meet this difficult burden of proof. On appeal, you are arguing that the court should have required you to prove your case only by a preponderance of the evidence. You could open your argument with a paragraph that begins with a topic sentence:

> The court should have required plaintiff Moore to prove her title by a preponderance of the evidence. Instead, it required proof by clear and convincing evidence. The court erred, because it misconstrued the requirement that plaintiffs must rely on the strength of their own titles and not on the deficiencies of a defendant's title.

This paragraph is a perfectly acceptable way to start out. It satisfies the most important requirement, stating your argument at the beginning. However, you would be more effective if you placed the topic sentence at the end:

> In property litigation, plaintiffs must rely on the strength of their own titles and not on the deficiencies of a defendant's title. Here, the court misconstrued this requirement and imposed on plaintiff Moore the difficult burden of proving her title by clear and convincing evidence. Instead, it should have required proof by a preponderance of the evidence.

The revised paragraph builds to its conclusion. It begins by discussing the general legal principle. It then becomes more specific and states the legal argument. Because the paragraph ends with the legal argument, the reader naturally expects the subsequent paragraphs to explain that argument more fully. The last sentence thus provides a transition to what follows.

The principle governing the introductory paragraph has a corollary respecting the concluding paragraph. When possible, the concluding paragraph should parallel the introductory paragraph. Write a concluding paragraph that builds to a conclusion and ends with the topic sentence. The topic sentence should be your conclusion. In this way, you reinforce the point you are arguing.

The corollary on concluding paragraphs is flexible. It works best in briefs. In other documents, other formats also can be effective. For example, here is the conclusion section of a law review article. The section begins with the article's conclusion, the results of an empirical study. It then places the results in context and ends with a very general conclusion to which the study results point.

Our study clearly shows that federal courts of appeals infrequently cite legal periodicals. Furthermore, most citations are to recent articles from a small group of elite journals.

This paucity of citations demonstrates the continuing tension in legal education resulting from two conflicting definitions of the enterprise. One definition identifies legal education as professional training. The other identifies it as an academic endeavor. Yet, citation studies demonstrate that legal scholarship makes only a modest direct contribution to the daily practice of law. Thus, the time has come to acknowledge that legal scholarship is overwhelmingly an academic endeavor of little immediate perceived value to the rest of the profession.[1]

[c] Give the Reader a Road Map

When you are setting out on a trip, you want to know your destination and how to get there. A road map helps. It identifies the roads on which you will travel, perhaps points out some landmarks, and shows you the location of your destination.

The reader is also setting out on a journey. At the outset, you can help him or her with an orientation by supplying a road map paragraph. In it, you tell the reader your conclusion, your argument, and the order in which you will present it. Without the road map paragraph, the reader may get lost and fail to learn what your conclusion is, much less your argument.

Here is an example. Crawley, the plaintiff, argues that the defendant bank wrongfully cashed a check with a forged indorsement and debited the amount from his account. You represent the bank. In moving to dismiss the complaint, you might submit a brief with this road map paragraph:

State statutes bar Crawley from bringing this action for two reasons. First, he failed to comply with the three-year statute of limitations for notifying a bank of an unauthorized indorsement. Second, he failed

---

[1] Louis J. Sirico, Jr. & Beth R. Drew, "The Citing of Law Reviews by the United States Courts of Appeals: An Empirical Analysis," 45 U. Miami L. Rev. 1051, 1056-57 (1991).

to comply with the four-year statute of limitations for bringing an action for conversion.

With this introduction, the reader knows that you will be making two arguments invoking two statutes of limitations, one for notifying the bank of an unauthorized endorsement and one for bringing a conversion action. The reader also expects you first to argue that Crawley waited too long to notify the bank of the unauthorized endorsement. Without the road map paragraph, the reader would not know what to expect next. The easier you make it for the reader to follow your argument, the more persuasive you will be.

Here is a more formal road map paragraph. It appears near the end of Part I, the introductory section of the *Report of the Association of American Law Schools Special Committee on Problems of Substance Abuse in the Law Schools*:

> The report is intended to provide both information and advice. Part II reports information concerning the nature and extent of the substance abuse problem in the legal profession and in the law schools. Part III describes efforts outside the law schools to deal with substance abuse—particularly the extensive initiatives undertaken by the legal profession and by the medical profession to attack similar problems. One of the lessons to be learned from the experience of the bar and the medical colleges is the overriding importance of confidentiality in substance abuse programs. For that reason, Part IV examines the need to assure students of the confidentiality of substance abuse counseling and treatment and to inform them about the use of that information in the bar admission process. Part V briefly reviews federal legislation applicable to the problem of substance abuse in the law schools. Part VI reports on existing law school policies and practices concerning substance abuse in general, and specifically on substance abuse by law students. Part VII discusses the problem of substance abuse by law faculty. Finally, Part VIII contains a set of recommended policies and programs that law schools should consider in order to deal more effectively with the problem of substance abuse.[2]

With so detailed a road map, the reader is very unlikely to get lost. However, the report's authors could have helped the reader further by better describing the destination, that is, including a brief summary of the committee's recommendations.

[d] Use Topic Sentences

As an advocate, you want to make certain that the reader understands every building block of your argument. The building blocks are the paragraphs. To construct sound building blocks, use topic sentences.

---

[2] 44 J. Legal Educ. 35, 37 (1994).

As you recall, a topic sentence states the main idea of a paragraph. It provides the topic of the discussion that goes on in the paragraph. Although most paragraphs have one topic sentence, some paragraphs may begin with two or three. In these cases, the topic sentences collectively state the one main idea of the paragraph, and the precise point of the paragraph appears in the final topic sentence before the discussion part of the paragraph begins. (If you have more than one point to make in a paragraph, you need more paragraphs. In each paragraph, you make only one point.)

In most paragraphs, the topic sentence is at the beginning. However, it sometimes appears at the end. As we discussed earlier in this chapter, you will want to place the topic sentence at the end of the introductory paragraph of your argument and of any major section of your argument.[3]

Consider this example. A criminal defendant has lost at trial and, on appeal, is arguing that he received ineffective assistance of counsel. In particular, the defendant argues that his attorney failed to present an alibi defense and put two alibi witnesses on the stand. You represent the attorney. If you were not conscious of the power of the topic sentence, you might write this paragraph:

> Two weeks before the defendant's trial, his attorney had used these two witnesses to present an alibi defense in the trial of co-defendant Thurman Carlton. The defense failed. The jury rejected the argument and convicted Carlton of first degree murder. However, at the defendant's trial, his attorney did not present the alibi defense. Nonetheless, despite ample evidence to convict him of other, more serious offenses, the defendant was convicted of only aggravated assault.

Without a topic sentence to give the paragraph unity and direction, the reader must figure out the point of the paragraph: presenting these witnesses would have been detrimental to the defendant. Even if the reader manages to correctly identify the point, you have weakened your argument in two ways. First, you have made the reader waste energy deciphering the paragraph so that he or she has less energy to focus on its argument. Second, you have deprived the paragraph of a sentence that could give your argument greater intensity.

Suppose that you decide to revise the paragraph and include a topic sentence. If you fail to place it at the beginning, you could end up with this result:

> Two weeks before the defendant's trial, his attorney had used these witnesses to present an alibi defense in the trial of co-defendant

---

[3] You may decide not to use a topic sentence when the general idea of the paragraph is clear, for example, in a narrative of the facts. However, when you are making this decision, exercise caution. By omitting a topic sentence, you risk making the theme of the paragraph unclear.

Thurman Carlton. The defense failed. The jury rejected the argument and convicted Carlton of first degree murder. Presenting the testimony of these alibi witnesses would have been detrimental to the defendant. At the defendant's trial, his attorney did not present the alibi defense. Nonetheless, despite ample evidence to convict him of other, more serious offenses, the defendant was convicted of only aggravated assault.

Here, the topic sentence is the second to last sentence. Until the reader reaches it, he or she does not know what you are arguing. Again, the reader is spending disproportionate energy determining the structure of the paragraph and has less energy to spend understanding your argument.

Suppose that this time, you revise and place the topic sentence first:

Presenting the testimony of these alibi witnesses would have been detrimental to the defendant. Two weeks before the defendant's trial, his attorney had used these witnesses to present an alibi defense in the trial of co-defendant Thurman Carlton. The defense failed. The jury rejected the argument and convicted Carlton of first degree murder. However, at the defendant's trial, his attorney did not present the alibi defense. Nonetheless, despite ample evidence to convict him of other, more serious offenses, the defendant was convicted of only aggravated assault.

Now you've got it right. By placing the topic sentence at the beginning, before the discussion part of the paragraph, you give the paragraph unity and direction. The paragraph becomes an effective building block of your argument.

As we discussed earlier, sometimes you need a group of topic sentences to state the point of the paragraph. In our example, suppose that you decide to include the defendant's argument in the paragraph. In that case, you will want to begin with an affirmative statement of your client's argument, raise the defendant's argument, and then refute it. (*See* Chapter 1, Part 3.) This strategy requires using three topic sentences:

In a singularly brutal rape-murder case, defendant's counsel employed effective vigorous strategies that resulted in only a fifteen-year sentence. The defendant argues that his counsel should have pursued an alibi strategy and placed two alibi witnesses on the stand. However, presenting the testimony of these witnesses would have been detrimental to the defendant. Two weeks before the defendant's trial, his attorney had used these witnesses to present an alibi defense in the trial of co-defendant Thurman Carlton. The defense failed. The jury rejected the argument and convicted Carlton of first degree murder. However, at the defendant's trial, his attorney did not present the alibi defense. Nonetheless, despite ample evidence to convict him of other, more serious offenses, the defendant was convicted of only aggravated assault.

As you can see, the point of the paragraph appears where it should be: just before the discussion begins, in the final topic sentence.

[e] When Appropriate, Recapitulate Your Point at the End of the Paragraph

Sometimes, you will find it effective to recapitulate your point at the end of the paragraph, particularly if you can do so with some flair. For instance in the last example, you might decide to end the paragraph with this additional sentence:

Had his attorney pursued the alibi strategy, the defendant might now be serving a life sentence.

Even if you are not creative enough to construct so appealing an ending, you may decide that you need a concluding sentence. An ending like this would be perfectly satisfactory:

If his attorney had pursued the alibi strategy, the defendant might have been convicted of a more serious offense.

[2] Put Your Best Arguments First and Develop Them More Fully

When we read a brief, report, court opinion, or other document, we usually pay more attention at the beginning. After a while, our interest wanes. In addition, we expect the important arguments to come first and to be developed in proportion to their importance. We can use this information to improve our advocacy. It tells us to place the most important arguments first and allocate more space to them.

To a great degree, which arguments are the most important depends on the facts of the case and the statutes and case law in your jurisdiction. However, there are some general principles that you can use. The most important is to emphasize your least radical arguments. A radical argument is one that requires a court to make new law or reject precedent. A court is far more comfortable ruling in your favor if you can persuade it that your argument is a generally accepted one and actually quite conservative.

Here is an example. Suppose that your client signed a prenuptial agreement when he was married and now is seeking divorce. Depending on its interpretation, the prenuptial agreement may be less advantageous to your client than a financial allocation under the state's equitable distribution statute. You have two possible arguments. First, the prenuptial agreement is unclear and open to interpretation. The better interpretation is the one that favors your client. Second, a prenuptial agreement that determines rights upon divorce is contrary to public policy and therefore void. Despite the agreement, the equitable distribution statute should apply.

Which argument should you put first and develop more fully? Clearly you should begin with the argument based on the interpretation of the prenuptial agreement. That argument is best, because it is the least radical. Courts are hesitant to invalidate an entire agreement or to decide a major social issue. They much prefer making a less momentous decision like interpreting a provision in a contract. Therefore, offer the court a reasonable, conservative way to decide the dispute.

The principle favoring nonradical arguments has numerous applications. Most notably, it leads you to prefer arguments that raise nonconstitutional issues over ones that raise constitutional issues. Whenever possible, courts try to avoid deciding cases on constitutional grounds.

As with all rules, sometimes you will decide to break this one. Sometimes the nature of the arguments and their relation to one another dictates the order in which you should present them.

For example, suppose your client is a defendant in an action for libel. You have two defenses. First, the statements are not libelous. Second, even if they are libelous, they are true. Your second argument is the strongest. However, if you place it first, your argument will not flow. If you begin with your first argument, you can start by explaining the law of libel and set the stage for the second argument. The solution: Place your first defense first and your second defense second. Nonetheless, develop your second defense as fully as if it were your first defense.

EXERCISES

1. Here are eight sentences. Please rearrange them to create two paragraphs. Make the first paragraph an introductory one that ends with a topic sentence. Make the second paragraph one that begins with a topic sentence. At the beginnings of some of the sentences, you may add introductory phrases and transitional words, for example: "According to the court," and "Therefore."

1. Butterwell cannot gain relief from the Equine Corporation simply because the assault he suffered took place on the sidewalk bordering Equine's building.

2. In this city, landowners do not control sidewalks; the city owns them.

3. A landowner has no duty to protect an invitee from incurring injury on property that it does not control.

4. An invitee died after being assaulted in a nearby parking lot that the defendant Chamber of Commerce did not own.

5. The decedent was not on property that the Chamber controlled, and, therefore, the Chamber owed him no duty of care.

6. In *Steinmetz v. Stockton City Chamber of Commerce,* the Court of Appeals confirmed that a tenant or landowner like Equine has a duty of care that extends only to the property it controls.

7. A defendant like the Chamber or Equine cannot be responsible for criminal conduct that takes place on property it does not control.

8. The Chamber had no right to station security guards on property it did not control, no right to place lighting in a parking lot other than its own, and no right to control the activities of its invitees or third paries occurring off the property that it controlled.

2. According to the United States Supreme Court, although the Eleventh Amendment prevents one state from suing another in federal court, it does not prevent one state from suing another in its state court. *Nevada v. Hall,* 440 U.S. 410 (1979). Here is a paragraph from Justice Blackmun's dissent in *Nevada v. Hall,* 440 U.S. at 429-30:

> The Court's expansive logic and broad holding—that so far as the Constitution is concerned, State A can be sued in State B on the same terms as any other litigant can be sued—will place severe strains on our system of cooperative federalism. States in all likelihood will retaliate against one another for respectively abolishing the "sovereign immunity" doctrine. States' legal officers will be required to defend suits in all other States. States probably will decide to modify their tax collection and revenue systems in order to avoid the collection of judgments. In this very case, for example, Nevada evidently maintains cash balances in California banks to facilitate the collection of sales taxes from California corporations doing business in Nevada. Under the Court's decision, Nevada will have strong incentive to withdraw those balances and place them in Nevada banks so as to insulate itself from California judgments. If respondents were forced to seek satisfaction of their judgment in Nevada, that State, of course, might endeavor to refuse to enforce that judgment, or enforce it only on Nevada's terms.

Please add a concluding sentence that recapitulates the point of the paragraph.

3. When your client took a shower at his apartment, he was scalded. The poorly-maintained hot water heater had raised the water temperature excessively high. The lessor points to an exculpatory clause freeing her from all liability, even in cases of negligence. You have two possible arguments. First, the clause can be interpreted to hold the lessor liable. Second, the clause is unconscionable and, therefore, void. All things being equal, which should be your primary argument?

4. While drunk, your client transferred her interest in her house to her former husband. You have two possible arguments. First, the transfer was fraudulently induced and, therefore, invalid. Second, the deed failed to satisfy certain significant formal requirements imposed by statute. All things being equal, on which argument should you rely most heavily?

5. Your grandparents gave land to the city so long as the city used it for a park. If the land were to be used for another purpose, it would immediately revert to the grantors. Four years ago, the city turned the park into a parking lot. You are your grandparents' successor to the possibility of reverter. You demand that the city return the land to you. However, the city points to a state statute requiring the owner of a reversionary interest to bring an action to quiet title or to eject the grantee within two years of the breaking of the condition.

You have two possible arguments. First, the statute constitutes an unconstitutional taking of property. Second, the statute does not apply to the facts of your case. All things being equal, on which argument should you rely most heavily?

ADOPT A PERSUASIVE WRITING STYLE

Thus far, we have discussed a general theory of writing persuasively and an approach to structuring your argument. With this chapter, we move on to specific techniques for making your substantive arguments strong. In this chapter, we present the three most powerful techniques for writing persuasive sentences and paragraphs:

(1) Be Concrete

(2) When You Want to Emphasize a Word or Idea, Place It at the End of the Sentence.

(3) When Appropriate, Use the Same Subject for a Series of Sentences.

[1] Be Concrete

Suppose that you represent Proudie, the plaintiff in a personal injury case. In your argument, you might write this sentence:

Proudie has established that his emotional injuries manifested themselves physically.

After some reflection, you might decide to rewrite it this way:

Proudie has proven that his emotional injuries caused coronary artery disease and a heart attack.

The rewrite permits you to make a more compelling case for your client. Consider the words that you changed. Instead of the abstract word "established," you used "proven," a concrete word with a connotation of activity. Instead of the abstract word "manifested," you used the concrete word "caused." Instead of describing the critical injuries with the vague and abstract word "physically," you identified them concretely as "coronary artery disease and a heart attack." The lesson: Write in concrete terms.

When you argue for a client, you are not arguing for an abstract legal principle. You are arguing for a decision that has practical consequences. In the same manner, judges are not interested in debating legal abstractions; they are interested in resolving specific disputes. When you write concretely, you drive home the fact that your case is not an academic debate, but a conflict involving real people.

Some lawyers use abstract words in the mistaken belief that they are achieving a lofty tone. However, the goal of persuasive writing should be a different one, to paint a graphic picture in the reader's mind. To achieve this goal, use the simplest language possible, use words that the reader is least likely to have to look up in the dictionary, and use words that describe things in concrete terms.

Here is another example. Your client, Nally, is bringing a false light invasion of privacy action against the *Rocky Hill News*. You are arguing that your client need prove only negligence, as opposed to knowledge of falsity or reckless disregard of the truth. Here is a sentence that might appear in your argument:

> In order for a private individual to recover compensatory damages in a false light invasion of privacy action against a media defendant, he or she should need to prove only that the publisher printed the statement negligently.

The sentence is unnecessarily abstract. See what happens when we revise it by merely including the names of the litigants.

> In order for a private individual like Nally to recover compensatory damages in a false light invasion of privacy action against a media defendant like the Rocky Hill News, he should need to prove only that the News printed the statement negligently.

Even this small a change makes the sentence far more concrete and more likely to hold the reader's attention. By being more concrete, we can make the sentence even more persuasive:

> In order for a private individual like Nally to win compensatory damages in a false light invasion of privacy action against a media defendant like the Rocky Hill News, he should need to prove only that the News acted negligently in stating that he sold contaminated vegetables.

In this rewrite, we made changes designed to make the sentence easier to understand and to create a feeling that Nally deserves compensation. We changed "recover" to "win" and "asserting" to "stating." We retained "compensatory damages," because it is a legal term of art for which there is not a better substitute. We used "contaminated" instead of "poisoned," because most readers use "contaminated" in every-day conversation, and some readers might find "poisoned" to overstate the facts and lose faith in our honesty. Most significantly, we included specific information about what the newspaper did. It made a damaging charge against a merchant that was bound to ruin his business.

Here is a final example. You represent Trinkets, a small store in a mall. Suburban Realty, the lessor, is demanding that Trinkets relocate to a part of the mall that will attract fewer customers. It argues that the lease gives it this authority. In your argument, you might include this sentence:

Accepting the lessor's construction of the lease would mean that the lessor has the right to move the lessee to a less desirable part of the mall.

Because the sentence is abstract, the argument is not as persuasive as it could be. The argument becomes stronger when we make the sentence more concrete:

Accepting Suburban Realty's interpretation of the lease would mean that it has the right to move its lessee, Trinkets, from a prime location to a part of the mall that would attract fewer customers.

We can make the sentence even more persuasive by making it even more concrete:

Accepting Suburban Realty's interpretation of the lease would mean that it has the right to move its lessee, Trinkets, from a prime location at the mall's entrance to the basement where it would attract fewer customers.

[2] When You Want to Emphasize a Word or Idea, Place It at the End of the Sentence

[a] To Emphasize Information, Use the End of the Sentence

In a sentence, the beginning and the end are the best places to put information on which you want the reader to focus. Use the beginning of the sentence for information that is already familiar to the reader. This information is usually the subject of the sentence. Also use the beginning for information that the reader expects or can understand easily. Use the end of the sentence for new information that you want to emphasize.

Using the end of the sentence for emphasis is almost intuitive. Jokes have their punch lines at the end. In mystery stories, we discover the culprit at the end. We like closure. For example, if you were organizing the American Revolution, which rallying cry would you pick:

It is tyranny to tax citizens who are unrepresented!

or

Taxation without representation is tyranny!

If you were Winston Churchill assuming the position of prime minister in war-time England, would you say:

Blood, toil, tears, and sweat are all that I have to offer you.

or

I have nothing to offer but blood, toil, tears, and sweat.

If you were Oliver Wendell Holmes, would you write:

Experience, not logic, has been the life of the law.

or

. The life of the law has not been logic: it has been experience.

To use a more conventional example, you might write:

It was an impermissible conflict of interest for the attorney to represent both defendants.

However, if you wished to emphasize that the attorney had a *conflict of interest*, you would do better to write the sentence this way:

For the attorney to represent both defendants was an impermissible conflict of interest.

You can extend this principle to clauses. The last clause in a sentence gets emphasis. For example:

The defendant failed to meet her burden, as the trial court held.

In this sentence, you emphasize that the *trial court* agreed with your assertion. However, you probably want to emphasize that the defendant had failed to meet her burden. If so, you would revise the sentence to end with the clause you wish to stress and with the word "burden":

As the trial court held, the defendant failed to meet her burden.

Even if you are writing a sentence in which you are not making a dramatic point, do not let it trail off. Instead, end it with a strong word. You want the reader to see you as confident and assertive. Sentences that trail off are not assertive.

[b] If Necessary to Make Use of the End of the Sentence, Forgo the Active Voice

Sometimes the only way to place the appropriate word at the end of the sentence is to pass up a strong active-voice verb in favor of a weak active-voice verb or the passive voice. Using the end of the sentence is such a powerful tool that most of the time you will decide to forgo the strong active-voice verb. Consider this example:

Assumption of the risk must be proven by the defendant.

To eliminate the passive voice, you might revise the sentence this way:

The defendant must prove assumption of the risk.

Although the second version may have a strong active verb, the sentence may not suit your purposes. If you wish to emphasize that the burden of proof is on the *defendant,* then the first version is more effective Thus you may decide to sacrifice the active voice in order to write more persuasively.

Here is another example:

> Although the Commonwealth has an interest in preserving the confidential relationship between a victim and her psychotherapist, that interest is overridden by the defendant's right to confront and cross-examine a hostile witness.

This sentence ends by emphasizing the defendant's right to confront and cross-examine. To keep that idea at the end of the sentence, you must use the passive-voice verb "is overridden." Replacing it with some active-voice verb like "must submit to" or "must succumb to" would leave you with a verb that fits less well in the sentence or possibly changes its meaning.

[c] To Emphasize More than One Word or Idea, Use a Semicolon or More Sentences

Suppose you find that you have too many words or ideas that you want to emphasize. You can accommodate them by creating more positions in your sentences that give emphasis. Use a semicolon or create more than one sentence.

Use a semicolon to connect two independent clauses that are so intimately related that they belong in the same sentence. The word before the semicolon and the word before the period will receive emphasis. Here is an example from Justice Harlan's dissent in *Poe v. Ullman*:

> Due process has not been reduced to any formula; its contents cannot be determined by reference to any code.[1]

By using a semicolon, Justice Harlan was able to emphasize two words: "formula" and "code." He also constructed a sentence that emphasizes the substantive parallelism of the clauses.

Creating more than one sentence is any easy way to emphasize more words or ideas. Suppose you are arguing that a court-appointed guardian should not have the right to terminate life-sustaining medical treatment. As a first draft, you might write this sentence:

> If there is a right to forgo medical treatment, the anomaly of vesting it in a third person should be avoided and the patient should exercise that right.

After thinking about your draft, you decide that you want to stress two points. First, the right to end medical treatment is the patient's. Second, to permit a guardian to make the decision would be anomalous. In order to emphasize both points, you must use two sentences.

> If there is a right to forgo medical treatment, the only person who may exercise that right is the patient. To vest the decision in a third person would be anomalous.

---

[1] 367 U.S. 497, 542 (1961).

In the rewrite, you end one sentence with "patient" and one with "anomalous." Thus you stress both your points.

[d] To Emphasize Information, Place It at the End of the Main Clause and Place the Main Clause at the End of the Sentence

By a main clause, we mean an independent clause, that is, a clause that could stand by itself as a complete sentence. For readers, the main clause is the one that receives the most attention. If you place the information you want to stress at the end of the main clause, you give it great prominence.

Suppose you are arguing that a witness's testimony is inadmissible. In your first draft, you might write this sentence:

> Her expert testimony was inadmissible, because her opinion addressed the complainant's general character as opposed to his truthfulness on a specific occasion.

If you wanted to emphasize the reasons for the testimony's inadmissibility, you might be satisfied with this sentence. However, if you want to emphasize that the testimony was inadmissible, you might revise the sentence this way:

> The expert's opinion addressed the complainant's general character, as opposed to his truthfulness on a specific occasion, making her testimony inadmissible.

Although this version places greater emphasis on the inadmissibility of the testimony, the message that you are emphasizing does not appear in the main clause. Therefore, you need one more revision:

> Because the expert's opinion addressed the complainant's general character as opposed to his truthfulness on a specific occasion, her testimony was inadmissible.

Now, with the main clause at the end of the sentence, you are making the best use of the sentence's structure to emphasize your point.

[e] To Deemphasize Information, Place It in a Dependent Clause That Is Not at the End of the Sentence

This lesson on emphasizing arguments has a corollary. Sometimes you want to downplay adverse information. To do so, do not place it at the end of the sentence and do not place it in the main clause. Instead, place it in a dependent clause that is not at the end of the sentence. Consider this example:

> The driver was responsible for his decision to drive drunk, although the passenger had purchased beer for him.

Suppose that you represent the passenger. You do not want to emphasize that the passenger bought beer for the driver. Nonetheless, it is a fact and it would be suicidal to ignore it and permit your opponent to point out your omission. Therefore, you need to include it, but deemphasize it. Keep the information in the dependent clause and place the main clause at the end of the sentence:

> Although the passenger had purchased beer for the driver, the driver was responsible for his decision to drive while drunk.

With this rewrite, you include the damaging information. However, you still emphasize to the reader that the driver bears the responsibility for driving drunk.

[3] When Appropriate, Use the Same Subject for a Series of Sentences

By using the same subject for a series of sentences, you make it clear that you are telling the story of the subject. As a result, you give a series of sentences unity and direction and reinforce your argument.

Suppose that your client is bringing an action for employment discrimination against her former employer, the Omega Corporation. She is bringing her action under the Employment Discrimination Act, which prohibits racial discrimination in the workplace. Once harassment occurs, the statute requires the employer to eliminate the misconduct by taking prompt remedial action. Your client argues that Omega failed to take this action. Her argument might include this paragraph:

> The inadequate response by Omega violates the Act. Although a prompt investigation is the first step an employer should take, Omega did not investigate the claims of harassment at the time of the first complaint. Omega's mere verbal reprimands were insufficient to stop the discrimination. Stronger steps were within Omega's power. Suspending, demoting, transferring, or firing the supervisor were possibilities. Moreover, Omega's corrective steps were so tardy that they did not take place until after the employer had been forced to leave the company. Omega thus failed to meet its statutory obligation.

Although you have made an accurate argument, you can make it far more persuasive. You need to paint an unfavorable picture of Omega. To achieve this goal, transform the argument into a story about Omega and its neglect:

> The Employment Discrimination Act prohibits racial harassment in the work place. Once harassment occurs, the Act requires an employer to take prompt remedial action to eliminate the misconduct. Here, Omega failed to take this step.

> With its inadequate response, Omega violated the Act. Although an employer should initially respond by promptly investigating the complaint, Omega failed to take this first step. When its verbal

reprimands proved insufficient to stop the discrimination, it failed to take stronger steps. Although it could have suspended, demoted, transferred, or fired the supervisor, it failed to ey .cise any of these options. When Omega finally took corrective steps, it acted so tardily that the employee had already been forced to leave the company. Omega thus failed to me ; its statutory obligation.

In this rewrite, whenever possible, the subject of each sentence and clause is either "Omega" or "employer." The rewrite makes it clear that you are discussing Omega's misconduct and detailing how it failed to comply with the statute. In this way, you present a compelling argument for employment discrimination.

This lesson may lead you to wonder if it prevents you from adding variety to sentences. Many of us were taught to vary the subject of the sentence to keep the reader from becoming bored. You might have been tempted to use various synonyms for Omega, for example, "the corporation," "the employer," and "the defendant."

This concern for variety is misplaced. You probably were not bored when you read the rewrite. If you had used synonyms for Omega, you might have confused the reader, who could wonder whether "Omega," "the corporation," "the employer," and "the defendant" all referred to the same entity. Because legal writing often requires the reader to struggle with difficult analysis, you want to make your sentences as unconfusing as possible. Do not sacrifice understandability for variety.

How do you add variety to your sentences? There are two effective methods. The first is to vary the length of your sentences. (You will find it particularly effective to end some paragraphs with a short sentence that has a punch line.) The second is to begin some sentences with phrases or dependent clauses.

For an illustration, look again at the second paragraph in the last example. In the six sentences, the main clauses all have the same subject. However, four begin with dependent clauses, and one begins with an introductory phrase. The first and last sentences are short; the rest are medium to long. These differences give the paragraph more than enough variety.

Sometimes the lack of variety adds to your effectiveness. For example, here is a perfectly acceptable paragraph:

On September 18, the eleven plaintiffs walked in front of a group of houses on Laurel Road. The signs they carried bore their message and were carried on the public sidewalk. They sang softly together, and no one was accosted, blocked, or touched. Nonetheless, they were jailed.

Here is a rewrite in which every sentence has the same subject, every sentence is short, and, with one exception, the first word of every sentence is the subject:

On September 18, the eleven plaintiffs walked in front of a group of houses on Laurel Road. They walked on the public sidewalk. They carried signs bearing their message. They softly sang together. They accosted no one. They blocked no one. They touched no one. They were jailed.

The parallel construction of each sentence makes this paragraph particularly compelling. Of course, if you were to write every paragraph this way, you would lose your effectiveness quickly. However, an occasional paragraph like this one is very striking.

EXERCISES

1. Please assume these facts:

   (a) Conway was an employee at a building site. At the time of the accident, he was standing on the steel frame of the building.

   (b) A crane unloaded building supplies on the building frame, and the frame collapsed.

   (c) Conway fell between nineteen and twenty feet. As a result of the fall, Conway fractured a vertebra.

   (d) As a result of the fall, Conway had three reconstructive surgeries. During one of the surgeries, a rod was implanted to support his backbone.

You represent Conway. Please rewrite this passage to make it more concrete and, therefore, more compelling:

> While Conway was executing his employment obligation on the frame of the building, a crane deposited materials on the frame for use in constructing the building. The frame collapsed, and Conway fell and incurred a fracture of his vertebra. Because of this event, he has been compelled to undergo reconstructive surgical procedures, including rod implant surgery.

2. (a) Please rewrite this sentence to emphasize that the landlord violated its obligations:

> The landlord violated its obligations, according to the trial court.

(b) Please rewrite this sentence to emphasize "changing circumstances" and "remove the condition." Hint: You may wish to use more than one sentence:

> The covenant may someday become unreasonable because of changing circumstances and permit the owner of the servient estate to remove the condition by successfully suing, even if the trial court approves the covenant's indefinite time limitation.

3. Using the lessons in this chapter, please rewrite this paragraph to make it more effective:

> The town ordinance is exclusionary and, therefore, invalid, as it applies to Broughton. Although land in the town is zoned for waste disposal, the property is unsuitable for this purpose. The municipality has thus made it impossible for Broughton to receive a permit from state authority, namely the state Department of Environmental Resources, to dispose of this commodity on property zoned for this purpose.

CHAPTER 4

STATE YOUR FACTS PERSUASIVELY

"The facts speak for themselves," wrote Demosthenes,[1] Euripides,[2] Plautus,[3] and Terence.[4] "Fools must be rejected not by argument, but by facts," wrote Flavius Josephus, the Judean general and historian.[5] "Facts are ventriloquists' dummies. Sitting on a wise man's knee, they may be made to utter words of wisdom; elsewhere they say nothing or talk nonsense," wrote British author Aldous Huxley.[6] According to a common-place among lawyers, cases are decided on the facts. Therefore, the lawyer should write the underlying factual narrative with a view toward persuading the reader to find for the client.

Despite the wisdom of the ages, a surprising number of lawyers have no idea how to make the facts of their case part of a persuasive argument. If you followed the example of many lawyers, you would present the facts in a neutral and tedious manner. If you followed the example of others, you would attempt to make the facts a part of your advocacy. However, you would do it in the wrong way. You would write in a flamboyantly opinionated style and frequently ignore adverse facts that your opponents were bound to point out.

Instead of imitating these bad examples, you should use your common sense: State the facts in objective language, but, nevertheless, put your best foot forward.

To illustrate the principles in this chapter, we use excerpts from the briefs submitted to the United States Supreme Court in *Hazelwood School District v. Kuhlmeier*.[7] In that case, students at Hazelwood East High School brought an action against the principal, the school district, and other individuals affiliated with the school system. The principal had censored articles in *Spectrum*, the school newspaper. The articles dealt with pregnant students and the divorces of the parents of students. In this litigation, the plaintiff-students argued that, for First Amendment purposes, *Spectrum* was a public forum. In a public forum, the First Amendment applies, and, under

---

[1] The Great Thoughts 104 (George Seldes ed. 1985) (De Falsa Legatione).
[2] Id. at 134 (Fragments).
[3] Id. at 338 (Aulularia).
[4] Id. at 410 (The Eunuch).
[5] Id. at 215 (Against Apion).
[6] Time Must Have a Stop 301 (1944).
[7] 484 U.S. 260 (1988).

the facts of this case, the students argued that it forbids censorship. Ultimately, the United States Supreme Court ruled against the students.

[1] Write Objectively, but Persuasively

Although the rules for presenting the facts in a case require avoiding value-laden words and opinionated writing, you still can use objective statements to advance your client's position. Here is an example.

In *Kuhlmeier*, the school board's attorneys argued that the board and the principal acted reasonably to protect the privacy of students and their families and to insure fairness to the divorced parents who were discussed in an article. Because of the rule about objective writing in the Statement of the Case (also called the Statement of Facts), the attorneys could not include in the Statement their opinion that the principal acted correctly in censoring statements that arguably violated the privacy of the parents. However, they made the point by objectively asserting facts. They employed this strategy by reproducing the words of students that appeared in the censored articles. For example:

My dad didn't make any money, so my mother divorced him.

My father was an alcoholic and he always came home drunk and my mom really couldn't stand it any longer. . . .

My dad wasn't spending enough time with my mom, my sister and I. He was always out of town on business or out late playing cards with the guys. My parents always argued about everything.

A less astute lawyer might have omitted the examples and written only a general sentence like this:

The newspaper included articles in which students discussed their parents' divorces.

Although this sentence conveys the same facts as the original, it does not send the same strong message: the student writers were invading the privacy of families and perhaps making untrue or unfair accusations.

The factual reporting in the original version is far more persuasive than rhetoric would have been. Even if the conventions of legal discourse permitted using rhetoric in the Statement of the Case, the school board's attorneys would have been wise to stick with the facts. If they had included the facts and then added a paragraph of rhetoric, they would have indulged in an extravagance that would have weakened the impact of the facts.

[2] Stress Favorable Facts and Deemphasize Unfavorable Facts

You must state all critical facts, whether they help or hurt your case. If facts are helpful, you want to make sure that they stand out for the reader.

If they are adverse, you want to make sure that they do not dominate your narrative.

For example, in *Kuhlmeier*, the school board's attorneys wanted to stress that the district court found in the board's favor. Of course, the attorneys could have merely mentioned the fact as they chronicled the case's procedural history:

> The United States District Court for the Eastern District of Missouri denied declaratory relief to the plaintiffs.

However, this sentence would have had no persuasive impact. It is a sentence that the opposing litigants might have used.

Instead, the school board's attorneys emphasized the district court's opinion in the second paragraph of the Statement of the Case:

> On May 9, 1985, after a three-day trial to the court, the Honorable John F. Nangle, Chief Judge, United States District Court for the Eastern District of Missouri, held respondent's First Amendment rights were not violated when petitioners prohibited publication of articles containing "personal accounts" of pregnant high school students and students' explanations of why their parents divorced. He found that petitioners reasonably acted to protect the privacy of the students and their families, to avoid the appearance of official endorsement of the sexual norms of the pregnant students, to ensure fairness to the divorced parents whose actions were characterized, and to limit the school-sponsored newspaper to materials appropriate for high school age readers.

Throughout the Statement of the Case, the board's attorneys quoted the district court's opinion extensively. By pursuing this strategy, they achieved three goals. First, they emphasized an important fact. Second, they made an appeal to authority—the opinion of the judge who was closest to the evidence in the case. Third, they permitted the judge's words to make the school board's argument for it.

An additional goal is to deemphasize adverse information. The school board's attorneys presumably wanted to downplay the fact that the controverted articles did not include the names of the students who were quoted. At the same time, they could not omit the fact. Their opponent surely would include it and possibly claim that the school board misled the court by ignoring it. Therefore, they buried this fact in a paragraph containing information damaging to the student plaintiffs:

> The student authors of the pregnancy profiles and "Divorce's Impact" story used questionnaires to research their articles. Each subject was told the information would be used in Spectrum. The three pregnant girls were told their names would not be used. They were

not given, however, any instructions regarding parental consent, and there was no evidence such consent was obtained. The parents of the students quoted in the "Divorce's Impact" article were not "contacted to explain or rebut the quoted statements of their children." App. A-39.

They could have buried the adverse information more deeply by rewriting the paragraph this way:

> The student authors of the pregnancy profiles and "Divorce's Impact" story used questionnaires to research their articles. The student subjects were not given any instructions regarding parental consent, and there was no evidence such consent was obtained. Each subject was told the information would be used in Spectrum. The three pregnant girls were told their names would not be used. The parents of the students quoted in the "Divorce's Impact" article were not "contacted to explain or rebut the quoted statements of their children." App. A-39.

To appreciate this strategy, consider how they might have written the paragraph:

> Each student quoted in the story was told the information would be used in Spectrum. Their parents were not contacted. However, the three pregnant girls were told their names would not be used.

This version contains the same information as the original. However, it leads off with damaging information and does not develop information favorable to the board as completely as it could have. As a result, the writer runs the risk that the reader will focus on the steps the students took to avoid any breaches of privacy.

[3] To Make Facts More Graphic, State Them in Detail

As the previous examples suggest, a way to emphasize a fact is to state it in detail. As readers, we assume that information receiving more space is more important than information receiving less space.

For example, the school board's attorneys argued that the newspaper was a classroom project completely under the school's control. To provide a factual basis for their argument, they might have written:

> The teacher selected the newspaper's staff, made decisions on such matters as publication dates, and worked closely with the students writing articles and laying out the paper.

Instead of settling for these generalizations, they adopted a more persuasive tack. To emphasize the degree of control, they quoted the district court's opinion, which set out the teacher's authority in great detail:

> [The teacher] selected the editor, assistant editor, layout editor and layout staff of the newspaper. He scheduled publication dates, decided

the number of pages for each issue, assigned story ideas to class members, counseled students on the development of stories, reviewed the use of quotations, edited stories, adjusted layouts, selected the letters to the editor, edited the letters to the editor, called in corrections to the printer, and sold papers from the Journalism II classroom.

[After a draft was completed, the teacher] would review the article, make comments, and return it to the students to be rewritten or researched further. Articles commonly went through this review and revision process three or four times.

In contrast, the students' attorney had to argue that the students enjoyed considerable independence in running the newspaper. Therefore, their brief should have detailed different facts. The brief might have included this passage:

The newspaper's chief editors made decisions on such matters as what articles to publish, when to publish, and when an article was ready for publication.

However, the brief draws greater attention to the critical facts by stating them in detail. Because the lower court's opinion was adverse, it cites alternative authority, the trial transcript:

The editor-in-chief and assistant editor made the decisions on what articles would be included in the paper, according to the advisor's testimony.

The student editors scheduled the publication dates, the number of pages and the number of issues according to the advisor. The editor-in-chief would check an article ready for publication to see if it had sufficient facts and research.

Cathy Kuhlmeier testified that as the layout editor, she wrote no stories, and her work for the paper consisted of selecting which stories would be included (along with her three staff members), what parts of articles would fit into the available space, and positioning them into the page size. She also indicated that the copy editors changed article content and the editor-in-chief and assistant editor told the staff members what an article should cover. There was no testimony that the advisor decided, changed or controlled content in any way. (References to transcript omitted)

Another use for detail is to emphasize the actions that someone failed to take. For example, in the amicus brief of the America Civil Liberties Union, the attorneys wanted to emphasize that the principal's decision to censor the newspaper was an automatic, unreasoned response. They made the point by noting the steps that a reflective decisionmaker might have taken:

The principal's decision to censor the six articles was made unilaterally and without any articulated reasons. He did not discuss his objections with the students or raise the possibility of editorial revisions. Indeed, he did not even inform them of his actions. The students first learned that two full pages of their newspaper had been cut when the paper was released.

Subsequently, the principal indicated that his concerns were limited to two articles . . . . Specifically, the principal feared that . . . . He also objected to . . . .

In these paragraphs, the attorneys listed sins of omission to subtly argue that the principal acted arbitrarily and only later invented rationales for his action.

[4] Include Statements of Opinion by Reporting the Opinions of Others

In stating the facts of your case, you cannot assert your opinion about those facts. However, you can insert opinions favorable to your client: Instead of stating your own opinion, report that someone else offered that opinion. In this way, you are stating a fact—what someone else stated—not your opinion. This technique is called "masked editorializing."

Kuhlmeier offers several illustrations. For example, the school board's attorneys wanted to argue that the teacher of the Journalism class had virtually complete control over the newspaper. Therefore, they quoted the words of the trial court:

The district court found that the teacher of Journalism II "both had the authority to exercise and in fact exercised a great deal of control over Spectrum," and "was the final authority with respect to almost every aspect of the production and publication of Spectrum, including its content."

Later on in the Statement of the Case, the attorneys reiterate the point, again by quoting the trial court:

The district court found "the most telling facts are the nature and extent of the Journalism II teacher's control and final authority with respect to almost every aspect of producing Spectrum, as well as the control or pre-publication review exercised by Hazelwood officials in the past."

The students' attorney might have countered these arguments by quoting the words of the opinion of the Eighth Circuit, which held in their favor.

In these examples, the attorneys make the essential points without rhetoric or value-laden adjectives and adverbs. Moreover, they do not berate the opposing party. Instead, they report the assertions of the court below. In this way, they state facts in an objective manner and still write as advocates. By placing their respective opinions in the mouths of authoritative third parties, they also make their arguments far more persuasive.

When you engage in masked editorializing, you are not limited to quoting the opinion of the court below. You might quote the testimony of a litigant, an expert witness, or other witness.

[5] Present Your Statement of Facts in an Orderly and Effective Manner

When you draft a Statement of Facts, think about how to gain and keep the reader's attention. If the initial paragraphs do not interest the reader, he or she may read the remaining paragraphs only casually and thus disregard an important part of your argument.

The typical lawyer begins the Statement of Facts by dryly reciting the case's procedural history. If you start with this introduction, you will have to work hard to gain the reader's interest. If you then unfold your narrative in chronological order, you will insure that the reader cannot identify the central issue until he or she has digested several paragraphs or pages. To improve your effectiveness, you need a better way to organize the Statement of Facts.

Begin your Statement of Facts with a single sentence that identifies the central issue and captures the reader's attention. In *Kuhlmeier*, if you were writing the school board's brief, you might begin your Statement of Facts with this sentence:

> This case concerns the right of a school system to exercise control over a school-sponsored newspaper in order to protect the privacy of students and their parents and to teach responsible journalism.

If you were writing for the student plaintiffs, you might begin with this sentence:

> This case concerns the constitutional right of students to publish a newspaper without censorship by school officials.

As you can see, each opening sentence identifies the issue from the viewpoint of the respective party. Although each sentence is ostensibly objective, each includes a strong element of advocacy.

Unless the case's procedural history is important to your case, it should not comprise the second paragraph. Because the procedural history usually is tedious and not critical, do not permit it to become a boring introduction to your narrative. Instead, present parts of it when they naturally arise in the course of your narrative, usually toward the end.

If you believe it important to present the procedural history at the beginning of the narrative, create a subheading entitled "Procedural History" and place the history under it. Then create a second subheading entitled "Facts" and proceed with your narrative. In this way, you present the procedural history at the beginning, but invite the reader to pass over it, if he or she wishes.

When you begin the narrative, you should consider leading off with an introductory paragraph or two that summarize the facts and intrigue the reader. If you were writing this sort of paragraph for the school board in *Kuhlmeier,* you might write it this way:

> At the Hazelwood East High School, the Hazelwood School district authorizes a course entitled Journalism II in which students learn to publish a newspaper and become responsible journalists. In May 1983, students in that class attempted to publish articles containing personal accounts of pregnant high school students and student explanations of why their parents divorced. The high school principal believed that these articles invaded the privacy of students and their parents and might be unfair to the divorced parents. Therefore, he refused to permit their publication. As a result, he faced litigation by certain disgruntled students in the Journalism II class.

If you were writing a similar paragraph for the plaintiff students, you might write it this way:

> For many years, students at Hazelwood East high School have published a newspaper, Spectrum. In May 1983, the principal disapproved of proposed articles on controversial subjects in the lives of contemporary teens, namely, divorce and teen age pregnancy. Therefore, he censored the newspaper. The student journalists brought this action and argue that the school has violated their First Amendment rights.

In both examples, the writers prepared the reader for what would follow so that the reader would be able to digest the narrative more easily. In addition, the writers summarized the facts from their respective client's viewpoint and thus contributed to the brief's persuasive power.

As you can see, with minimal effort, you can organize your Statement of Facts so that it is highly accessible to the reader. If you write factually, but still write as an advocate, the accessibility of your narrative will make it a compelling part of your argument.

EXERCISES

1. Here are the facts of an automobile negligence case. Jack Chadwick struck and injured John Bunce, a six-year-old boy. John and his mother are bringing an action for personal injuries and medical expenses. They argue

that Chadwick failed to keep a proper lookout and should have either stopped driving or driven more slowly when he had extreme difficulty seeing the street in front of him. You represent John. Please use this information to write a statement of facts favorable to him.

1. At 7:30 p.m., daylight saving time, on July 8, John Chadwick was driving along Hogglestock Road at approximately 20 to 25 miles per hour.

2. At 7:30 p.m., it was still daylight. Sunset was at 7:40 p.m.

3. The police report states that no improper driving was indicated, that Chadwick had been driving at approximately 20 to 25 miles per hour, and that 25 miles per hour was the maximum safe speed under prevailing conditions.

4. On Chadwick's right side, the south side of the road, was a row of commercial buildings with diagonal parking. On the left side was a residential area. There was no cross street or pedestrian crosswalk in the vicinity.

5. John Bunce, a six-year-old boy, was playing with other children near the curb on the left hand side and ran into the path of Chadwick's car.

6. According to the police report, the car's skidmarks were 38-feet long, and the impact could have occurred anywhere within the 38 feet. At the end of the skid, the left wheel marks were 20 feet from where the south curbline would have been if there had been no parking area.

7. The impact broke the glass of the vehicle's left headlights and caused a dent in the front of its left front fender.

8. The only eye witnesses were Chadwick, John, and Harry, John's eight and one-half-year-old brother, who was one of the children playing there.

9. Harry testified that while he was watching another boy, who had fallen off his bicycle, he noticed that John had left and "he was about more than halfway across the street and I said 'John, watch out.' He started to turn around, but he didn't get all the way turned around and the car hit him."

10. John testified: "I didn't see the car before I started across the street. Then I heard my brother calling me and yelling 'Watch out!' I started to turn around, but it was too late. I saw the car coming at me."

11. Chadwick testified:

I didn't see him until after I hit him, because the sun was glaring off the cars that were parked on the side of the road there and it was hard to see. The glare came from the cars parked in the shopping center and from the cars coming toward me and anything that would glare. When I struck the boy, I was driving where I should have been, near the middle of the road. When I hit the brakes, it was the same time that I hit him. I couldn't see the other side of the street, because there were so many cars backing in and out of the shopping center there and cars coming from the opposite direction. I was trying to look in all directions to make sure there was nothing there. Then I heard a thud and saw the kid rolling down the street. When I heard the thud, I guess simultaneously I hit the brakes and turned to the right. That was it.

2. Please refer to Exercise 1. You are Jack Chadwick's lawyer. Please write a statement of facts favorable to him.

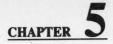

MAKE EQUITY AND POLICY ARGUMENTS

[1] Argue More Than the Law

In most cases that go to trial, and certainly in most cases on appeal, both parties have sound legal arguments. Therefore, if you argue only the law, you run a strong risk of losing. If you want to improve your odds, you must argue more than the law. You must argue the equities and social policy.

To argue the equities means to argue that your client is the most sympathetic litigant and should win as a matter of justice. For example, your client parks her car in a large parking lot and returns later only to discover that her car has been stolen. On her behalf, you sue the parking lot and probably argue that it breached its duty as a bailee. To argue the equities, you would emphasize that your client was a captive customer of the parking lot; she had no other safe place to leave her car. She thus was forced to entrust her car to the defendant and ultimately found that the trust was betrayed.

If you represent the parking lot, you also should make an argument on the equities. You would argue that your client makes a good faith effort to run a secure parking facility. However, your client knows that complete security is not possible. Therefore, it posts large signs and prints on its tickets a notice that disclaims liability and instructs its customers to lock their cars.

As the example illustrates, arguing the equities does not necessarily require making an impassioned plea for justice. In facts, these sorts of pleas can work against you if they sound exaggerated. Here, as in other types of persuasive writing, the best strategy is a slightly understated argument backed by compelling facts. Make the court aware of your client's plight. However, avoid the heavy rhetoric.

To argue policy means to argue that the holding you seek has beneficial consequences for society and the holding that your opponent seeks does not. For an example, we can return to the case in which your client's car was stolen from the parking lot. To bolster your legal argument with a policy argument, you might state that a parking lot has a duty to meet the legitimate expectations of customers that their cars will be safe. A decision favoring your client will send an important message to parking lot owners.

If you represent the parking lot, you might argue that requiring parking lots to guarantee fail-safe security would make their insurance costs prohibitive or make insurance unavailable. As a result, public parking could become exorbitantly expensive or even nonexistent.

As you can see, the equity argument focuses on the particulars of a case and attaining a fair result for your client. In contrast, the policy argument generalizes about what the case's outcome might mean for society. In our example, the equity arguments of the competing litigants pit fairness to the car owner against fairness to the parking lot. The policy arguments pit encouraging the parking lot industry to be more responsible against saddling that industry with a debilitating financial burden.

Of the two types of arguments, we believe that equity arguments are more persuasive, especially in the lower courts. However, your best strategy is to use both equity and policy arguments. It will be difficult for a court to reject your position if you can show that not only has it the backing of the law, but it also accords with fundamental notions of fairness and benefits society.

Now that we have introduced equity and policy arguments, we will use more examples to gain experience with them. Most of our examples will come from the illustrative case we used in Chapter 4, *Hazelwood School District v. Kuhlmeier*.[1] In that case, students in a high school journalism class produced *Spectrum,* the school newspaper. When the principal censored controversial articles, the students brought a legal action. They argued that *Spectrum* was a published forum in which the First Amendment forbade the principal's censorship.

[2] Make Equity Arguments

In *Kuhlmeier,* the students' advocates could have focused exclusively on the legal argument. They could have referred to leading cases to define a public forum and then argued that cases finding a public forum had facts similar to the facts here. They could have argued that cases not finding a public forum were distinguishable.

Of course, the opposing lawyers would present their own legal argument. They would conclude that the case law did not support classifying a high school newspaper as a public forum. As for cases supporting the students, they would distinguish them on the facts.

To increase the odds of prevailing, the attorneys should introduce equity arguments favoring their respective clients. For example, the school board's attorneys might have stressed that treating the newspaper as a public forum would interfere with their efforts to teach students to be responsible journalists and adults. They might have included a passage like this one:

---

[1] 484 U.S. 260 (1988).

The school created the newspaper not as a public forum, but as a teaching vehicle. Instead of adopting a hands-off policy toward the newspaper, the school used it to instruct students in responsible journalism and citizenship. In the current controversy, the school was teaching students not to invade the privacy of others, not to risk charges of defamation, and to avoid hurting others for the sake of cheap sensationalism. To achieve these goals, they necessarily had to exercise some content control.

As for the plaintiff-students' equity argument, the attorneys filing an amicus brief for People for the American Way argued that the school created a limited public forum for expressive activity. Therefore, they emphasized the extensive freedom that the student editors and writers enjoyed. To make the argument stronger, the attorneys created empathy for the students by showing how much they were benefiting from publishing the newspaper. As part of this equity argument, they quoted the Eighth Circuit's opinion:

> Spectrum was not just a class exercise in which students learned to prepare papers and hone writing skills, it was a public forum established to give students an opportunity to express their views while gaining an appreciation of their rights and responsibilities under the First Amendment to the United States Constitution and their state constitution.[2]

In both examples, the equity arguments are not merely general appeals for empathy. Both examples refer to the legal issue: whether the newspaper is a public forum. By tying the equity argument to the legal argument, they make the legal argument more persuasive.

[3] Make Negative Equity Arguments

So far, we have discussed using equity arguments to create empathy for your client. However, you also can make a "negative equity" argument in which you portray the opposing litigant or some third party in an unfavorable light.

In *Kuhlmeier*, the students' attorney used this technique in describing the conduct of the principal. In the next paragraph, the attorneys portrayed the principal as intruding in a setting in which he did not belong, dispossessing the teacher, and violating curricular rules:

> Until this case arose, [the] . . . journalism curriculum did not include the principal. One day he usurped the teacher's role, replaced himself as advisor and changed the teacher-advisor position into that of editor.

---

[2] *Kuhlmeier v. Hazelwood School District*, 795 F.2d 1368, 1373 (8th Cir. 1986), rev'd, 484 U.S. 260 (1988).

He then directed that only four pages of the students' work be distributed at school. These actions were not consistent with the Curriculum Guide, were not inherent in the previous pattern of classroom activity and were contrary to the purpose of journalism education as adopted by Hazelwood.

Be careful not to overemphasize the opposing party's shortcomings. The negative strategy can backfire by leading the reader to dismiss your characterization as overblown and therefore unreliable. After losing faith in your credibility on the equities argument, the reader may lose confidence in the credibility of your legal analysis.

Although the negative equity strategy can be effective, you usually will have more success with emphasizing the equities that favor your client. Accentuating the positive is more persuasive than emphasizing the negative.

[4] Make Policy Arguments

Although policy arguments deal at a more abstract level than equity arguments, they still should relate to the facts of the case. The facts should provide an example of how the holding you seek would advance sound policy.

For example, in *Kuhlmeier*, the school board's attorneys had to counter the student argument that the newspaper was a public forum. To bolster their legal argument, they made the policy argument that a public forum is inconsistent with the pedagogical function of a school. More specifically, they argued that the court should not interfere with the running of a high school:

> The public secondary school classroom is not a competitive market of ideas wherein diverse thoughts compete for the allegiance of a discriminating audience. The secondary school classroom involves a highly selective presentation of ideas and expression as dictated by the course curriculum. The purpose is to convey information to, and inculcate societal values in, minors. The state as teacher must have the authority to select what information is conveyed and by whom.

The students' attorney might have written a corresponding paragraph like this one:

> As a public forum, a high school newspaper plays an important educational role. The classroom is a place for conveying information and ideas in accordance with a course curriculum. However, the larger educational experience exposes students to a competitive market of ideas and teaches them to make discriminating choices. For this educational mission, a newspaper is a potent teaching tool. As a forum

for diverse ideas and opinions, it challenges students to make the sorts of evaluations we expect of responsible citizens.

In each example, when the reader considers the policy argument, he or she thinks of it in the context of Hazelwood East High School. Because the reader ties the policy argument to the specifics of the case, the argument makes the litigant's position more persuasive.

[5] Combine Equity and Policy Arguments

If an equity or policy argument can increase your persuasiveness, imagine how you can strengthen your argument by combining equity and policy arguments.

Combining the two is not difficult. As we have seen, equity and policy arguments have much in common. Equity arguments necessarily deal with the facts of the case, and, to be effective, policy arguments must relate to the facts. Because the arguments share this quality, you can easily use both in the same paragraph.

For example, in its amicus brief supporting the students in *Kuhlmeier,* the People for the American Way argued that the school officials violated the First Amendment by interfering with the right to receive information. In making the argument, its attorneys combined equity and policy arguments:

> Although only the putative speakers are before the court, broader interests are at stake. In silencing respondents—student journalists who sought to address important social issues in the pages of Spectrum—petitioners placed an obstacle in the road to knowledge for members of the larger high school community, impermissibly contracting the spectrum of available knowledge.

In this passage, the attorneys appealed to the equities by making the student journalists attractive: the students tried to do something that was beneficial, and they were silenced. At the same time, the attorneys integrated the policy argument: censorship is wrong, because it impermissibly contracts the spectrum of available knowledge.

The format of the paragraph is not the only one that the attorneys could have used. Here is another possible way to present the equity and policy arguments:

> Censorship of a student newspaper impermissibly contracts the spectrum of knowledge available to a high school community. This nation's constitutional commitment to freedom of speech and the press militates in favor of declaring a newspaper to be a public forum. Otherwise, at schools like Hazelwood East High School, administrators preferring conformity to informed debate will ban newspapers like

Spectrum when student journalists seek to address important social issues.

In this version, the paragraph begins with a policy argument, the importance of free expression. It then concludes with an equities argument that serves as an example of why the policy argument is so important.

Here is another example, this time from *Boos v. Barry*, 485 U.S. 312 (1988).[3] In that case, the petitioners challenged a District of Columbia statute forbidding critical political demonstrations near the official buildings of foreign governments. In their brief, their attorneys argued that the statute violates the First Amendment, because it failed to leave open alternative channels of communication for the petitioners' message:

> The First Amendment also requires that restrictions of public forum speech "leave open ample alternative channels for communication of the information." *Clark v. Community for Creative Non-Violence*, 468 U.S. 288, 293 (1984).

The attorneys then supported this legal argument with a policy argument that quoted an earlier United States Supreme Court case:

> As explained in *Young v. American Mini-Theatres, Inc.*, 427 U.S. 50, 76 (1976) (Powell, J., concurring):
>
> The primary concern of the free speech guarantee is that there be full opportunity for expression in all of its varied forms to convey a desired message.

To further bolster the legal argument, the attorneys introduced an equities argument to demonstrate how important this requirement is to individuals like their clients:

> Petitioners are individuals of no great means. They are not supported by political action committees and cannot afford to buy radio or television time or pay for newspaper ads. Their ability to communicate depends largely upon effective picketing—a unique mode of communication. The anti-picketing provisions of § 1115 apply everywhere within 500 feet of the perimeter of any official foreign building. . . . If Petitioner Waller is allowed to protest against the backdrop of the Nicaraguan Embassy, his message will be conveyed effectively and likely will attract attention. But if he is relegated to holding his "STOP THE KILLING" sign in from of a Burger King restaurant some 500 feet away, he may be perceived as either a vegetarian or an eccentric; and the effectiveness of his message will be severely impaired.

The attorneys thus strengthened the legal argument by beginning with a very general policy argument concerning free speech. They then added

---

[3] 485 U.S. 312 (1988).

an illustrative equity argument showing why the legal and policy arguments were particularly significant to citizens of limited financial means. By combining these different types of arguments, they permitted a synergism that strengthened their persuasiveness.

[6] Do Not Separate the Equity and Policy Arguments from the Legal Arguments

A common error by lawyers is to place the legal arguments in one section of a document and the equity and policy arguments in other sections. For example, in all too many briefs, the writer develops the various legal arguments and then tacks on an additional section that states the policy arguments. The attorney apparently expects the readers to remember the legal arguments and later to link them up with the respective policy arguments. Alternatively, the attorney assumes that a single all-purpose policy argument is sufficient to support the various legal arguments.

When you make a legal argument, integrate the equity and policy arguments. In this way, you insure that the reader will make the connections among the arguments. In addition, instead of offering one very general equity argument and one very general policy argument for the entire document, you can tailor these arguments to the specific legal argument you are making. Many of the examples in this chapter serve as illustrations.

EXERCISES

1. Please assume these facts. The plaintiff, Martha Dunstable, sustained injuries after Clara Van Siever hit her while driving under the influence of alcohol. Before the accident, Dunstable and Van Siever, both minors, attended a party, which was the scene of intoxication and underaged drinking. During the course of the party, Allingtown police answered two calls in response to neighborhood complaints about the party. However, they took no corrective action. Sometime later, an intoxicated Van Siever entered her car parked along the street, backed it up, and hit Dunstable who was standing in the street behind it

Dunstable brought a tort action against the Borough of Allingtown under the state's Municipal Tort Claims Act. The Act waives governmental immunity for "a dangerous condition of streets" when the condition "created a reasonably foreseeable risk of the kind of injury that was incurred." For there to be a waiver, the government must have had actual or constructive notice of the dangerous condition "at a sufficient time before the event to have taken measures to protect against the dangerous condition."

Dunstable argues that, under the Act, the borough is liable, because it created a dangerous condition when its police failed to stop underaged drinking and failed to stop individuals from driving while intoxicated. The borough responds that "dangerous condition" refers to conditions like potholes and not the circumstances in this case. Therefore, the borough argues, sovereign immunity protects it from liability.

You represent Martha Dunstable. Please list the persuasive equity and policy arguments you could make.

2. Please refer to the facts in the first question. You represent the Borough of Allingtown. Please list the persuasive equity and policy arguments you could make.

3. Until recently, Alexandra Repolsky lawfully resided in the United States as an alien. She came to this country to escape political and economic upheaval in her native country of Bohemia. Repolsky's elderly parents remain in Bohemia; however, her three sisters live in the United States as lawful permanent residents.

When Repolsky first came to the United States, she tried to find a job as an accountant, a field in which she had worked in Bohemia. Unable to find a position, Repolsky decided to borrow money from a loan shark, a common practice in Bohemia. The loan shark, Tobias Makker, was rumored to be a member of an organized crime family.

When Repolsky was unable to earn enough money to pay back the loan shark, Makker threatened her life. Repolsky offered to work as an accountant for Makker if he would forgive her loan. Makker agreed. While working for Makker, Repolsky discovered that he was not paying income taxes on all his annual income. However, because she was concerned that he might harm her, she continued to work for Makker even though she was aware that she might also be charged with tax evasion.

Eventually, Makker and Repolsky were charged with tax evasion and were convicted. Repolsky was sentenced to serve a one-year term in a minimum security prison. However, her sentence was later reduced to 500 hours of community service providing free tax advice to low income individuals. After Repolsky completed her required community service, she continued to provide these services. In the meantime, Repolsky met and married a United States citizen. They now have two young children, both born in the United States.

The United States Immigration and Naturalization Service (INS) has issued an order of deportation against Repolsky, because she committed a "crime involving moral turpitude." However, under applicable law, the INS will consider equitable and policy factors to determine whether it might be in the best interest of the United States to grant her a waiver of deportation.

You represent Repolsky. Please list equity and policy arguments that favor your client.

4. Please refer to the facts in the last question. You represent the INS. Please list equity and policy arguments that favor your client.

5. In violation of federal criminal law, your client Diane Shouldan presented false information to the Environmental Protection Agency in a bid application. She originally submitted the incorrect information at her employer's instruction, but later expressed concern about it to him. Two weeks later, she was fired for "lack of loyalty."

You argue that the dismissal should be treated as a wrongful discharge. Ordinarily, employers can fire employees for any reason or no reason. There is an exception to this idea of at-will employment: when a discharge violates an express public policy. As part of your brief to the trial court, you draft these paragraphs:

> An at-will employee cannot be terminated for refusing to violate a public policy stated in a statute. *Adams v. Cochran & Co.* In *Adams,* an employee lost his job because he refused to drive a company truck that did not conform to safety regulations. The court found that the exception to at-will employment applied when an employee was "forced to choose between risking criminal liability [and] being discharged from his livelihood."

> The *Adams* court held that the exception must involve a "statutorily declared public policy." The facts as presented do not indicate a clear situation in which Shouldan was given a choice of complying with orders that would require violating a statute or discharge. The fact pattern might suggest more a situation in which she was terminated in retaliation for expressing reluctance to continue to obey such instructions in the future.

> The primary strength of Shouldan's case is the weight of the circumstances leading toward a holding by the court that a favorable finding would comply with the policy advocated in *Adams.* The gravamen of *Adams* is to alleviate danger to employees put in a position of either violating the law (and public welfare) or losing their livelihood, and Shouldan's complaint clearly falls under this policy.

> A growing body of persuasive scholarly opinion supports finding the wrongful termination exception under at-will employment. Professor Blades examines the issues involved in the coercive power employers might wield and how that power can potentially lead to abuse. The "prime source" of this power, Blades states, is the absolute right of discharge found under the at-will doctrine. This right of discharge can be used to terminate for any cause, including "for cause morally wrong." Blades finds that the scope of the employer's appropriate control over the employee is impossible to define with precision.

When this control involves violation of statute or public policy this is perhaps of most immediate concern to the judiciary. An employer imposing a course of action upon an employee that constitutes potentially criminal behavior threatens basic social goals and values. Many of our rights and privileges are vulnerable to abuse through an employer's power.

A note in the Harvard Law Review also looks at tort cases finding that the defendant employer's conduct toward the employee undermines some important public policy. Cases of this type extend back to as early as 1959. *Peterman v. Teamsters Local 396.* In *Peterman,* plaintiff/employee allegedly lost his job for refusing to commit perjury. The California Court of Appeals reasoned that the employer's conduct jeopardized the policy of encouraging full and honest testimony. Though they have construed it very narrowly, a number of other courts have recognized the existence of the public policy exception.

The Harvard note states "these decisions indicate an increasing dissatisfaction with the at-will doctrine. The policy and doctrinal basis of the original common law rule has . . . been superseded by modern contract and tort principles that require revision of the doctrine."

Please rewrite this passage to strengthen and better integrate your equity and policy arguments. You may need to restructure the original substantially to achieve an appropriate level of integration and make the argument persuasive.

USE PRECEDENT PERSUASIVELY

Although Oscar Wilde declared that "consistency is to the life of the intellect . . . a confession of failure,"[1] most of us, including judges, like the stability and predictability that consistency offers. Judges like their decisions to be consistent with past decisions of their court. They also must be persuaded that their decisions are consistent with those of any higher court. In legal analysis and argument, being consistent means following precedent. Justice Oliver Wendell Holmes once wrote: "We believe the weight attached to [precedent] is about the best thing in our whole system of law."[2] Invoking precedent is a powerful tool of persuasion.

The difficulty with invoking precedent arises when the earlier case does not support your position or a court cannot clearly determine whether it supports your position. You might argue that the earlier case was wrongly decided. However, this tactic would work at cross purposes with your desire to claim that you are arguing consistently with existing case law. Therefore, an argument rejecting precedent should be an argument of last resort. Your first argument should be that existing law supports your position or, at least, is consistent with it.

In this chapter, we first review ways to select the most favorable precedent. We then discuss two ways to deal with seemingly adverse precedent: interpreting case holdings broadly or narrowly, as appropriate, and distinguishing cases on their facts. Finally, we explain how to deal with adverse precedent without sounding defensive.

[1] Rely on Favorable Precedent

The rules for invoking favorable precedent are easy enough. Give the most attention to cases in your jurisdiction with fact patterns similar to yours. If you cannot find these cases, find others with parallels to your case, preferably in your jurisdiction. Here are some general rules:

(1) Rely most heavily on cases from higher courts in your jurisdiction dealing with issues and facts closest to those in your case. Discuss those cases fully.

---

[1] Hesketh Pearson, Oscar Wilde: His Life and Wit 171 (1946).

[2] "Summary of Events," 7 Am. L. Rev. 558, 559 (1873); "Value of Precedent," in Justice Oliver Wendell Holmes: His Book Notices and Uncollected Letters and Papers 34-35 (Harry C. Schriver ed., 1936).

(2) Rely on cases with facts and issues close to yours that come from the court to which you are arguing. Discuss those cases fully.

(3) Discuss cases in your jurisdiction with issues and facts related to yours. The more that a case parallels yours, the more you should discuss it.

(4) Discuss cases from other jurisdictions that are parallel to your case. If most jurisdictions follow the rule or application you advocate, label it the majority position. If most courts or many prestigious courts have adopted your position in the recent past, label it the trend of law. If there is a leading case, discuss it fully.

(5) When you are documenting a majority position or trend of law, you may use long string citations. In other situations, you should avoid them and generally stick to the most recent leading cases. When you use string citations, consider following each cite with a parenthetical that briefly describes the case. For example: *Union County v. Hoffman,* 512 N.W.2d 168 (S.D. 1994) (permitting the abatement of a nonconforming use—here, a trailer park—that is a public nuisance).

(6) If no direct precedent addresses your case and the law is unsettled, support your argument with the cases and other authorities that seem most relevant. Cases from your jurisdiction should receive the most discussion. You probably will need to cite many cases and authorities and give them careful attention.

These rules would gain the agreement of most skilled legal writers. However, the difficult problems arise when precedent does not support your argument. Either the earlier cases are ambiguous or they appear to go against you. To these troublesome matters we next turn our attention.

[2] Interpret Precedent Narrowly or Broadly, As Appropriate

Most holdings are open to more than one interpretation. When dealing with precedent, select the interpretation that furthers your case. Depending on the facts of your case, you will choose to interpret the holding narrowly or broadly.

Here is an example of how to interpret a holding narrowly. Double D Demolition was an independent contractor working for Developmental Properties. When Double D Demolition acted negligently in demolishing an adjoining building, our client, Triple P. Realty, suffered damage to its office building. Because Double D was grossly underinsured, our client can collect for only a fraction of the damage it suffered. To receive full compensation, it must successfully sue Developmental Properties. However, a leading case in our jurisdiction, *Majestic, Inc. v. Alford,* holds that an employer is not liable for the negligence of an independent contractor.

Under this reasoning, Developmental Properties would not seem to be liable for the negligence of Double D.

To successfully sue Developmental Properties, we must differentiate *Majestic* from our case. We might attempt to distinguish the cases on the facts by arguing that Double D was not an independent contractor, but an employee. If that argument has no chance of prevailing, we might distinguish *Majestic* by interpreting it narrowly this way:

> In a case like this one, an employer is liable for the negligence of a financially irresponsible contractor. Although *Majestic, Inc. v. Alford* correctly states the rule that an employer is not liable for the negligence of an independent contractor, it applies that rule to a case in which the contractor was financially responsible. In contrast, the present case concerns a contractor who was grossly underinsured. Hiring a financially irresponsible contractor is tantamount to hiring an incompetent contractor, and, as other courts have held, renders the employer liable.
>
> The policy underlying *Majestic* and the argument here is the same: to assure that the burden of loss falls on the appropriate party and not on the victim. In *Majestic,* the burden properly fell on the contractor, since the employer had hired an independent contractor who carried the standard liability insurance. However, here, Developmental Properties failed to make certain that Double D had the proper insurance coverage. Developmental Properties was in the best position to assure financial responsibility and to avoid imposing the burden of loss on Alford, an innocent victim. Developmental's breach of duty renders it liable.

In interpreting a holding narrowly, you cannot rely on an arbitrary rationale for the way that you read the case. Your rationale must make sense. In this example, we focused on a factual difference between the cases—whether or not the respective contractors were adequately insured—and argued that the *Majestic* court meant its holding to apply only when a contractor carried adequate insurance. We backed up this reading with a policy rationale concerned with placing the burden of loss on the appropriate party. Without the policy rationale, our interpretation of the case would not persuade a court.

Here is an example of how to interpret a holding broadly. Our client is Lilian, a five-year-old. When Bernard, an eight-year-old, continually rode his bicycle close to Lilian in a threatening way, Lilian threw a rock at the bicycle and unintentionally hit Bernard in the eye. Bernard brought an action for battery. In your jurisdiction, the case of *Gresham v. Courcy* found a battery when a five-year-old boy punched another boy in the eye.

We could try to distinguish *Gresham* on the facts by arguing that Lilian is a girl and the defendant there was a boy. However, the distinction is not a persuasive one, particularly because of the general belief that girls mature more quickly than boys. We could distinguish the facts by noting that the *Gresham* defendant aimed the punch at the plaintiff while Lilian aimed it at the bicycle and missed. Unfortunately, standard tort law would not recognize this distinction and would hold Lilian liable.[3] Therefore, this argument would require us to seek a change in very traditional law.

The better approach is to read the *Gresham* holding broadly to require determining on an individual basis whether a child can form the requisite intent to commit a battery. Our argument might read this way:

> As the *Gresham* court held, tort liability arises when a child realizes the injurious consequences of his or her conduct. Following *Gresham* requires determining a child's mental capacity on an individual basis. In *Gresham,* the court upheld a finding that a five-year-old boy was liable, because he realized the injurious consequences of punching another boy in the eye. However, here, Lilian, the young girl, lacked the maturity to understand the consequences of throwing a rock at a bicycle. Moreover, at her age, she could not understand that in aiming a rock at a bicycle, she might hit its rider in the eye.

With this argument, we reject the narrow holding that *Gresham* found five-year-olds to have the mental capacity to commit battery. Instead, we argue for the broad holding that, although a five-year-old may have the capacity, a court must make an individual determination about each child. In our argument, we argue that having this capacity requires the ability to understand the consequences of one's action. Because the argument sounds sensible, it has a chance of succeeding.

Here is another example. In July, our client, Eames, stopped paying his monthly rent when the air conditioning unit in his apartment broke and Framley, the landlord, failed to repair it. In *Thorne v. Barchester,* our state's supreme court found an implied warranty of habitability in residential leases. In that case, the tenant did not have to pay rent, because the landlord failed to repair conditions that violated the local housing code. In our case, however, the housing code does not require a landlord to provide air conditioning.

The landlord's lawyer will argue that *Thorne* applies only when the landlord violates the housing code. To succeed, we must counter this narrow reading with a broad one. We might introduce our argument like this:

> As the *Thorne* court held, a landlord implicitly warrants that the leased premises pose no threat to a tenant's health and safety. Just as

---

[3] See W. Page Keeton et al., Prosser and Keeton on the Law of Torts § 9, at 39-40 (5th ed. 1984).

the housing code violations in *Thorne* threatened the health and safety of the tenant, the lack of air conditioning during a hot urban summer threatens the well being of tenants like Eames.

In this example, we cited *Thorne* for a very general holding. We treated the precise holding—the landlord has a duty to insure that residential property will satisfy housing code standards—as only an example of the general duty that a landlord owes a tenant. We then argued that maintaining an air conditioning unit is so similar to meeting housing code standards that it also falls within the landlord's general duty.

[3] Argue that Adverse Precedent is Distinguishable on the Facts

One way to harmonize adverse precedent is to argue that the contrary case is distinguishable from your case on its facts. If possible, go one step further and argue that the case really supports your position: Argue that the policy underlying the case is the one you are advancing.

Here is an example. Suppose that we work for the state's attorney-general. The state's Clean Water Act requires obtaining a permit before depositing dredged soil in intrastate waters. The Omnium Corporation is preparing to dump dredged soil into wetlands that do not adjoin intrastate waters.

In *State v. Silverbridge, Inc.*, the state's highest court has held that the statute applies to wetlands adjoining intrastate waters. However, Omnium relies on another high court case, *State v. Barsetshire, Inc.*, which held that the statute did not apply to a wetland that did not adjoin intrastate waters.

We seek to enjoin Omnium. To succeed, we must distinguish *Barsetshire* on its facts. We might make our argument this way:

> Just as wetlands adjoining intrastate waters affect the water quality and aquatic ecosystems of those waters, certain wetlands not adjoining them have the same effect. Because the goal of the Clean Water Act is to restore and maintain the chemical, physical, and biological integrity of this state's waters, the Act applies to both types of wetlands.
>
> As *State v. Silverbridge, Inc.* holds, achieving the Act's goals requires defining "waters" to include adjoining wetlands. Because the nonadjoining wetlands in this case affect water quality by trapping undesirable pollutants and sediments before they reach the waters, they are functionally the same as adjoining wetlands. Unlike the non-adjoining wetlands in *State v. Barsetshire, Inc.*, which had no drainage function or ecological connection with interstate waters, the wetlands here are critical to maintaining water quality. Therefore, the Act applies here.

This passage begins by arguing that both the policy and case law favor finding that the Act covers the wetlands here. Only then does it distinguish the adverse precedent.

This strategy avoids the need to reject the adverse case as wrongly decided and to ask the court to reject precedent. Instead, it argues that the policy and case law underlying the statute support finding that, in our case, the Act covers the wetlands. In the context of the argument, distinguishing *Barsetshire* on the facts seems logical and far from extreme.

Here is another example. A state statute requires a landlord to give a tenant at will thirty days notice before ending the tenancy. In *Griselda v. Alexandrina,* a court has held that residents of rooming houses are tenants at will. Our client is a hotel that is trying to terminate the stay of one of its guests without having to wait thirty days. Our initial strategy should be to distinguish our case from *Griselda*:

> Because a hotel guest is a licensee, a hotel can terminate the guest's stay without giving notice. Although *Griselda v. Alexandrina* interprets § 1.202 to require giving thirty days notice to the resident of a rooming house, that holding does not reach hotels and their licensees. As the *Griselda* court noted, the statute balances the landlord's rights as a property owner with the tenant's expectation of some degree of permanency. Roomers legitimately expect to enjoy a certain permanency of occupancy. Hotel guests do not. Therefore, the statute applies to roomers and not to hotel guests.

As you can see, this paragraph distinguishes *Griselda* on its facts by differentiating between a rooming house and a hotel. Moreover, it offers a legitimate reason why the distinction should make a difference here: roomers have an expectation of staying longer than do hotel guests. By looking to the legitimate expectations of the defendants in each case, it argues that the same policy rationale should underlie both cases.

[4] Deal with Adverse Precedent in a Positive Way

As we have emphasized, to be persuasive, you must present your arguments in an affirmative way. This principle applies when you are dealing with adverse precedent. If you deal with contrary arguments in a defensive way, the theme of your opponent's argument will dominate. If you want your theme to dominate, you must take an assertive stance.

For example, consider the last illustration, which distinguished rooming houses from hotels. Note that the sample paragraph makes the argument by presenting it in a positive way and not seeming to be on the defensive. However, suppose the preceding paragraph read this way:

> In *Griselda v. Alexandrina,* the court interpreted § 1.202 to require giving thirty days notice to the resident of a rooming house. The court

noted that the statute balances the landlord's rights as a property owner with the tenant's expectation of some degree of permanency. According to the court, its interpretation of the statute was proper, because roomers legitimately expect some degree of permanency. However, *Griselda* is distinguishable from the present case, because a hotel guest is a licensee and not a tenant. Moreover, unlike roomers, hotel guests do not enjoy an expectation of permanency. Therefore the notice requirement should not apply to hotels and their licensees.

Although this paragraph makes the same argument as the preceding one, it is not as persuasive. It leads off by presenting the opposing arguments and only then does it try to distinguish the hotel's case. As you can see, it is better to present your argument in an affirmative way and then introduce and deal with any contrary argument.

To further examine the principle of writing in a positive way, look at the other examples in this chapter. In each, the passage begins by emphasizing the writer's argument and only then taking on the opponent's argument.

Here are the first two sentences of each of the first four examples in this chapter. After each, we have placed a revision showing what the first two sentences might have looked like if the writer had adopted a defensive posture. The originals begin by stating the writer's theme and only then analyze the adverse precedent. As you will see, they illustrate the better way to present a persuasive argument.

Assertive: In a case like this one, an employer is liable for the negligence of a financially irresponsible contractor. Although *Majestic, Inc. v. Alford* correctly states the rule that an employer is not liable for the negligence of an independent contractor, it applies that rule to a case in which the contractor was financially responsible

Defensive: In *Majestic, Inc. v. Alford*, this state's highest court held that an employer is not liable for the negligence of an independent contractor. Developmental Properties relies on *Majestic*, because Double D was an independent contractor; however, *Majestic* may not control here.

Assertive: As the *Gresham* court held, tort liability arises when a child realizes the injurious consequences of his or her conduct. Following *Gresham* requires determining a child's mental capacity on an individual basis.

Defensive: As the plaintiff argues, *Gresham v. Courcy* found a battery when a five-year old child punched another child in the eye.

According to the plaintiff, the defendant here, like the defendant in *Gresham,* is liable, because a five-year-old realizes the injurious consequences of her conduct.

Assertive: As the *Thorne* court held, a landlord implicitly warrants that the leased premises pose no threat to a tenant's health and safety. Just as the housing code violations in *Thorne* threatened the health and safety of the tenant, the lack of air conditioning during a hot urban summer threatens the well being of tenants like Eames.

Defensive: In *Thorne v. Barchester,* this state's supreme court found that a landlord implicitly warrants that the rental property meets housing code standards and agrees to repair conditions that violate the code. As the landlord here maintains, the housing code does not require air conditioning; nevertheless, the *Thorne* holding should be extended to cover air conditioning and any other conditions that pose a threat to the tenant's health and safety.

Assertive: Just as wetlands adjoining intrastate waters affect the water quality and aquatic ecosystems of those waters, certain wetlands not adjoining them have the same effect. Because the goal of the Clean Water Act is to restore and maintain the chemical, physical, and biological integrity of this state's waters, the Act applies to both types of wetlands.

Defensive: Omnium, Inc. relies on *State v. Barchester,* which refused to find the Clean Water Act applicable to a wetland not adjoining intrastate waters. However, in that case, the wetland had no drainage function or ecological connection with intrastate waters.

EXERCISES

1. Five years ago, George Walker agreed to pay Anne Prettyman $500 monthly for the remainder of her life. Walker has stopped making payments, and Prettyman has brought an action at equity for specific performance. Walker argues that equitable relief is inappropriate, since Prettyman has an adequate remedy at law.

Your jurisdiction has two relevant cases. In *Gazebee v. Fothergill,* the court held that the non-breaching party to a continuing contract could gain equitable relief. In *Crofts v. Dalrymple*, the court held that the non-breaching party to a five-year contract had an adequate remedy at law and could not seek equitable relief.

Here is one way to write Walker's argument:

> As Prettyman argues, *Gazebee v. Fothergill* held that a nonbreaching party to a continuing contract could gain equitable relief, because specific performance would avoid the possibility of the parties relitigating the issue in the future. However, the adequacy of a legal remedy is supported by *Crofts v. Dalrymple*. There the court found that for the breach of a continuing five-year contract, the remedy at law would be sufficient, because the doctrines of res judicata and collateral estoppel would bar multiple and extensive litigation. The logic of *Crofts* should apply here, despite the *Gazebee* holding.

Please rewrite this paragraph to make it more persuasive.

2. Please refer to the facts in the first question. Here is one way to write Prettyman's argument:

> In *Crofts v. Dalrymple,* the court found a legal remedy adequate for breach of a five-year contract. Underlying the *Crofts* decision was the reasoning that a legal remedy was adequate, because a party is not likely to again breach a contract so limited in duration. However, here, the contract is of an unlimited duration and a later breach is quite possible. As *Gazebee v. Fothergill* holds, a nonbreaching party to a continuing contract, like Prettyman, is entitled to equitable relief, because it avoids the possibility of the parties relitigating the issue in the future. Once a court orders specific performance, there is no need for a plaintiff to bring a new action. The plaintiff need seek only enforcement of the existing order. Therefore, to avoid multiple and extensive litigation, an equitable remedy is necessary.

Please rewrite this paragraph to make it more persuasive.

3. Please assume these facts:

(a) Scatcherd is president of the Sowerby Corporation.

(b) Sowerby furnished Scatcherd with an automobile to use for business, pleasure, or convenience.

(c) Sowerby paid for all the gasoline used in the automobile.

(d) On June 1, Scatcherd was driving the automobile on a personal errand and hit Fillgrave, a pedestrian.

(e) Fillgrave has brought a negligence action against Sowerby. Fillgrave argues that Sowerby is liable under the doctrine of respondeat superior: when a servant operates a master's vehicle with the master's permission, the master is liable.

(f) In *Moffat v. Greshamsbury,* Greshamsbury was the vice-treasurer of Desmolines, Inc.

(g) Desmolines furnished Greshamsbury with an automobile to use for business, pleasure, and convenience.

(h) The cost of gasoline was allocated between Greshamsbury and Desmolines so that Desmolines paid for only the gasoline used on business.

(i) Greshamsbury was driving the automobile on a personal errand and hit Moffat, a pedestrian.

(j) Moffat brought a negligence action against Desmolines under the doctrine of respondeat superior.

(k) The court found that although Greshamsbury was liable, Desmolines was not.

You represent Fillgrave. You argue that the Sowerby Corporation should be liable. Please write a brief summary of your argument and deal with the adverse precedent of *Moffat v. Greshamsbury.*

CHAPTER 7

WRITING FOR NONLEGAL AUDIENCES

In their eagerness to get their thoughts onto the page, even experienced writers, and those who carefully prepare for oral advocacy by writing out their arguments, sometimes forget precisely what their goal is when they sit down to write a persuasive document. If you are trying to persuade a nonlegal audience, you may be hoping to persuade a client to retain your services, a jury to decide in favor of your client, or a lawmaking body to adopt or reject a specific proposal. To accomplish this goal, you must use the tools discussed in this book in ways that will be most effective with your particular audience.

[1] Writing for Clients

For purposes of this discussion, assume that the clients you need to persuade are lay clients, unsophisticated in legal processes and analysis. If your clients are sophisticated general counsel or corporate officers who have extensive experience with lawyers, your approach should more nearly approximate that suggested in the next chapter for communicating with other lawyers.

When you communicate with lay clients, consider the expectations and hopes those clients probably have for communications from their lawyers. Several likely expectations come to mind:

* Reassurance

* Demonstration of competence

* Clarification of the procedural status of the matter, and explanation of what happens next

* Clear explanation of applicable law

* Presentation of available options and consequences

* Predictions about how matters are likely to be resolved

* Demonstration of concern for the client as a person

* Clear explanation of fees and costs

* Respect for the intelligence and contributions of the client

This list demonstrates the complexity of the client's needs and expectations and the difficulty of meeting them all. Whether you are trying to persuade a client to accept a settlement, adopt some other specific course

of action, or merely trying to persuade the client that you know what you
are doing and are taking good care of the client's matter, every communication with a client has persuasion as a goal. How do we accomplish this
difficult task? Here are three suggestions:

* Use Appropriate Language

* Provide Useful Information

* Inspire Confidence

[a] Use Appropriate Language and Provide Useful Information

Use language the client will understand and provide only details that will
have significance to lay clients. Although technical legal language and the
details of legal processes and authorities may be necessary to persuade
other lawyers or judges, they will only confuse and frustrate your clients.
For example, suppose you are writing to your client about the possibility
of entering into a plea bargain. You wish to explain the process thoroughly,
and thus your first draft might look like this:

> Before you plead guilty to a lesser charge, you should be aware of
> what exactly plea bargaining means; the nature of the crimes with
> which you were charged; the nature of the lesser offenses with which
> you could be charged; and the consequences of plea bargaining. Plea
> bargaining is the process whereby the accused and the prosecution
> negotiate a mutually satisfactory disposition of the case. Before a court
> can accept a guilty plea, it must first make sure that you enter the plea
> with a complete understanding of the nature of the charge and the
> consequences of your plea. There are basically four kinds of pleas.
> You can plead not guilty to the entire indictment; you can plead guilty
> to the entire indictment; where two or more offenses are charged, you
> can plead guilty to one or more, but not all, of the offenses charged
> or guilty to a lesser offense with respect to any or all of the offenses
> charged (providing that there is a factual basis for the crime); or you
> can plead not responsible by reason of mental disease or defect. In plea
> bargaining, you should be prepared to concede some or all of your
> guilt in exchange for certain sentencing concessions. However, you
> must be advised that the prosecutor may recommend a specific
> sentence. This, however, does not cabin the judge's discretion, unless
> he or she previously agreed to the proposed plea. Plea bargaining is
> not a constitutional right. Thus, as I stated earlier, it is my best
> judgment based on the history of prosecutors, the nature of the offense,
> and your background, that the prosecutor will plea bargain.

This example uses terminology the average client will find difficult to
understand, and it provides far more detail than the client really needs or
can process at this point. If the client has specific questions, you can address

them in a subsequent letter or in a personal conversation. With this in mind, you might revise your draft to read this way:

> Before we begin discussions with the prosecutor, I would like to offer a brief explanation of what plea bargaining means and what its consequences are. Plea bargaining is a negotiation between the prosecutor and the accused. The goal is to reach a mutually satisfactory agreement that resolves the charges without the need for a trial. Before a court can accept a guilty plea that results from plea bargaining, it must first make sure that the accused completely understands the nature of the charge and the consequences of the plea.
>
> When we talk to the prosecutor, we will discuss both the offenses to which you may plead and the appropriate sentence. If you decide to plead guilty, you may plead guilty to some or all of the offenses charged or to a lesser offense that may be included. In plea bargaining, you should be prepared to concede some guilt in exchange for sentencing concessions. The prosecutor may recommend a specific sentence or the judge may use his or her own discretion.

Here is another example of a letter that is almost guaranteed to leave the client with more questions than it answers. It casually tosses around legal jargon and concepts without explanation and has a stream of consciousness flow that suggests the writer was thinking the problem through for the first time as the letter was being written. These characteristics are highly unlikely to encourage client comprehension or create trust in the lawyer.

> Once again, to address recovery against Mr. Walker, there is still the issue of his negligence. Negligence is a cause of action that will allow a victim to recover against an individual who has committed a legally recognized wrong. If you would like me to continue with your case, I will send you another letter that goes into more detail about following this theory for recovery. I must tell you though that because you were not wearing your seat belt, you may be regarded as being contributorily negligent in causing your own injuries. I must research that issue to find out if our state is a comparative negligence jurisdiction. If it is, your amount of recovery will be reduced or barred based on how much you contributed to your own injuries. In light of this issue, you may want to consider whether it is worth going ahead with this claim or seeking an alternative recourse with Mr. Walker.

Here is a rewrite that the client should have a better chance of understanding. It simplifies the language, does not throw around concepts the client may or may not be familiar with (or that the client may not even need to understand), and clearly lets the client know what the lawyer is thinking and intends to do next.

> We may sue Mr. Walker on the basis of his negligence. A victim of negligence may recover against an individual who committed a

legally recognized wrong. Thus we must show that Mr. Walker caused the accident by doing something careless or illegal. Because you were not wearing your seat belt, a court may decide that you had a role in causing your own injuries. I must research that issue to find out whether a court in this state might decide that you should receive less money or no money because you were not wearing your seat belt.

[b] Inspire Confidence

The client needs to believe that you are competent and that you have the client's best interests at heart. If you cannot convey these messages, you may not have many clients to represent. For example, suppose you are explaining to a potential client how you will handle the client's problem and what your services will cost. Feeling a little uncertain because of your inexperience, you might draft this paragraph:

> At this point I have tried to give you a general idea of where you are with regard to the law and the penalties you face. Considering the severity of the charges levied against you, it is inappropriate at this time for me to advise you as to a definite course of action. As we discussed at our meeting, if you wish to obtain my services, I will need a $500 retainer check before I proceed. This check will be deposited in an escrow account and drawn upon at a rate of $100/hour. Please be aware that a case of this magnitude will probably be time consuming. However, realizing that you are not a wealthy woman, I will see to it that the initial $500 covers you at least up to the point where I can advise you as to a definite course of action.

There is no reason to rewrite this paragraph—it should never have been written in the first place. While you must discuss fees with a prospective client, you should not ask a client to part with $500 when you seem to be saying that the case may be too complex and serious for you to handle with any degree of assurance.

Tell your client what $500 will buy. Presumably, you will use the initial five hours to conduct research and perhaps begin negotiations with opposing counsel. Then you will be ready to advise your client on a course of action. If this is your plan, state it in your letter. By presenting a concrete plan, you will promote confidence in your abilities.

Here is another example. Suppose you represent a client charged with embezzlement. You are advising him that a defense he has suggested will fail. You might draft this paragraph:

> You have expressed what you consider may be a viable defense to these charges. You stated that you originally began stealing the money as an act of retaliation against the bank, because bank officers ignored some alleged sexual harassment charges you asserted against a female executive vice president. Unfortunately, my research did not uncover

any evidence that retaliation for ignored sexual harassment charges is a viable defense to any of your criminal charges. Although you felt that it would be your way of compensating yourself for the alleged abuse, there is no guarantee that a court would have believed your story and awarded you any compensation. Thus, I disagree that this is a viable defense and may only be considered by the judge as being a reason for your actions.

After reading your draft, you would recognize its shortcomings. Although it explains that the law does not support the client's proposed defense, it does not demonstrate an understanding of the client's perspective. Therefore, it will not contribute to a good rapport with the client. You might revise the letter this way:

> You have offered a defense to these charges. You stated that you originally began stealing the money as an act of retaliation against the bank because bank officers ignored sexual harassment charges you asserted against a female executive vice president.
>
> Unfortunately, the law does not recognize retaliation for ignored sexual harassment charges as a justification for committing criminal acts. Although you felt that you were compensating yourself for the alleged abuse, the law requires that you pursue legal action in order to receive compensation. We can still pursue such an action if you would like to.
>
> In addition, even though the sexual harassment will not be a defense to the criminal charges, the judge or the prosecutor may consider it in imposing a sentence or negotiating a plea bargain. I will certainly raise the sexual harassment with the prosecutor and the judge.

Here is a final example. In this letter, the lawyer seems to think the client can handle his own case.

> First, your concern about the robbery is understandable. However, under the circumstances and without more information, I cannot in good conscience advise you as to the relative strength of your position. Your possible legal vulnerability notwithstanding, a minimum showing of four basic elements would be required for Ms. Graves to be successful against you. A successful demonstration of negligence on your part by Ms. Graves requires that 1) you had a clearly identifiable duty to protect tenants from harm outside of your building; 2) you breached (failed to fulfill) your duty to protect; 3) she suffered actual harm or damage; and 4) your failure to protect was the causal link to her suffering harm.

What is the client likely to think upon receiving this letter?: "Am I liable or not? What was I going to pay this lawyer for anyway?" After reading this letter, the client will not have much confidence in the lawyer. You should not give clients definite answers when you do not have them; however, at least you should explain how the elements of the law might apply to the client's situation.

Clients are a crucial audience. You must persuade your clients that you are the kind of lawyer they can trust to handle some of the most difficult and significant events of their lives. An essential part of a successful legal career is learning to communicate with clients in a way that they can understand and that inspires their confidence.

[2] Writing for Juries

The concept of "writing" for juries may seem a little strange at first, since you will be dealing with them only in making oral presentations during a trial. Nevertheless, if you do not write out your thoughts in some organized, coherent manner before you walk into a courtroom, you are unlikely to be very effective or persuasive. The importance of persuading juries cannot be overstated, yet such communication is not something we do well: "[A] jury trial is very often much like watching a foreign movie without subtitles," observes *Wall Street Journal* legal editor Steven Adler. "If there's a lot of action, you have a general idea what's going on. If there isn't a lot of action, you're in trouble."[1]

Trials are often conducted in a language that is needlessly alien to the jury. According to Adler, who has been observing trials and talking with jurors, jurors often have difficulty with such words as "ambiguously," "representation," "conversion," "tacitly," "nucleus," "executing," "artifice," and "immaterial," words with which lawyers are comfortable and which they use regularly. "Sometimes [jurors] ask for dictionaries, and usually the judge does not permit them to have a dictionary. They are simply seeking a definition of the word that they can understand so they can make use of it."[2] Because the judicial system has failed to remedy the communications chasm between the jury on the one hand and the judge and attorneys on the other, it continues to impair the jury's ability to do justice.[3]

This chapter is intended to help you formulate the written notes that will guide your oral presentations to juries. As we did when thinking about writing for clients, let us identify some expectations juries are likely to have. They expect lawyers to:

---

[1] "Panel One: Judge-Jury Communications: Improving Communications and Understanding Bias," 68 Ind. L.J. 1037, 1038 (1993) (reprinting Proceedings of the Annenberg Washington Program Conference, April 10, 1992: Communicating with Juries).

[2] Id. at 1039.

[3] See Fred H. Cate & Newton H. Minow, "Communicating with Juries," 68 Ind. L.J. 1101, 1118 (1992).

* clearly explain the facts and the law
* offer a comprehensible theory of the case
* make the case interesting
* respect the intelligence of the jurors and the importance of their function
* make jurors want to return a verdict in favor of your client

To help fulfill these expectations, use appropriate language and explain concepts clearly and concretely.

[a] Use Appropriate Language

As when writing for lay clients, you must communicate with juries using language that simply and clearly communicates the concepts you are trying to convey and not lapse into excessive legal jargon. Clear language is particularly important for juries, because they have to process what you are saying by listening to it. They do not have the opportunity to go back for a second look at a passage they found particularly difficult or troubling.

Consider this portion of the prosecutor's opening statement in the trial of a legislator charged with corruption. It might work well in a hornbook or treatise. How would you communicate the same information to a jury?

The crime of embezzlement is committed when a person comes lawfully into the possession of property, and afterwards and while it is in his possession forms and carries out the purpose of taking it for his own use. The evidence will show that the defendant:

* knowingly and willfully stole, embezzled and converted to his own use and to the use of others
* without authority
* funds of the United States well in excess of $100
* which had come under his control because of his position as a member of Congress.

Further, in embezzling the items and funds, the government will show that the defendant committed other crimes. The evidence will show that the actions of the defendant constituted the following additional crimes: mail and wire fraud, conspiracy, concealing material facts, and obstruction of justice.

You need to simplify the language and thus increase the likelihood that the message will be received. Here is one possible rewrite that avoids legal jargon and explains what the government intends to prove in plain English.

The crime of embezzlement is committed when a person gets property legally, and afterwards decides to take it for his own use. The government will show that the defendant knowingly and willfully embezzled funds of the United States well in excess of $100, which came under his control because of his position as a member of Congress.

Further, the government will show that the defendant committed other crimes, including mail and wire fraud, conspiracy, concealing material facts, and obstruction of justice.

[b] Explain Concepts Clearly and Concretely

If a jury is to understand and remember a point, the lawyer must make the point simply and, if possible, in a way the jury can actually "see." Using concrete language and images allows the jury to organize information in a way that makes it easier to retain and use when the time comes to evaluate the evidence.

In an opening statement, a lawyer must "package" the case so the jury can understand the significance of the evidence that is about to be presented. The lawyer also should provide an idea of the roles of the various participants in the trial, including the jury. Put yourself on the jury that hears this portion of an opening statement.

Ladies and gentlemen, my job is to present evidence, in the form of both documentation and live testimony, before you. My opposing counsel will do the same. Your job is to listen to all the evidence, from both sides, and weigh the credibility of each document and witness. In other words, my job is to put the pieces of the puzzle in front of you, piece by piece, sometimes bigger ones. Your job is to decide what pieces you believe and disbelieve from each side's case. At the conclusion of my case in chief, the defendant will present evidence. Once again, your job will be the same. You must choose Cain from Abel. At the end of these presentations, I will come forward again, and attempt to explain how all these pieces fit together. My opposing counsel will explain what puzzle or lack thereof she believes is formed. Ladies and gentlemen, the evidence will develop over these next few weeks, and, at the conclusion, I will ask you to think about everything and return verdicts against the defendant of guilty as charged on all the counts alleged.

Confused? What images played through your mind as you read this statement: weighing evidence? doing a puzzle? reflecting on biblical characters? Were they helpful or distracting? Did you understand what your role was or what the roles of counsel were? Compare this opening in the same case.

Your Honor, Counsel, ladies and gentlemen of the jury. My name is _____. I work for the United States Department of Justice. I am a prosecutor. This trial will unfold today like the pages of a book. Consider my remarks here as the table of contents. The book has characters—the defendant, his family, his colleagues. Many of these characters will testify for you today. This testimony makes the pages of the book—and the facts of this case. The book has a story. A real life story. A story about crime. A course of criminal conduct, spanning not one year, not five or even ten years, but twenty years. Twenty years of conspiracy and theft . . .

Ladies and gentlemen, the facts of the case will be painfully clear. It is my sad duty to present the government's case, chapter by chapter. It is for you, the jury, to do the much more important task, the writing of the final page and, as the defendant's secrets are revealed, line by line, you will see that this book can have only one ending. The final paragraph must mark the conviction of the defendant.

The second example is much clearer; it evokes only one image—reading a book—and it carries that image throughout the discussion. The language is clear, simple, and concrete. The image is not distracting; it helps you visualize how the parts of a trial fit together and what functions the prosecutor and the jury serve.

What image(s) do you get from this passage?

In terms of sheer magnitude, the hiring of ghost employees was the defendant's most egregious act. The defendant, on a regular basis, would turn in to his payroll officer a payroll sheet that did not describe the duties performed by his employees.

So, what did the sheet describe, you might ask?

Does this version seem clearer?

The hiring of numerous ghost employees was the defendant's most offensive act. The defendant, on a regular basis, turned in to his payroll officer payroll sheets for these employees. On the sheets, the spaces for describing the employees' duties were blank.

This version does not require that the jury already have the lawyer's knowledge about how the payroll sheets were designed, and what information they were supposed to contain. The jury gets a much clearer picture of a deliberate effort on the part of the defendant to conceal the fact that his "employees" were doing no work.

[3] Writing for Lawmaking Bodies

Lawmaking bodies—including legislatures and administrative agencies—may be particularly difficult audiences to write for. You are likely to be facing individuals with a wide variety of experience and expertise and the possibility of private or political agendas that you must consider. How do you persuade such a diverse group to do something? You must be clear, you must rely on arguments that are likely to have broad rather than partisan appeal, and you must convince the group that your proposal deserves to be given priority when there are likely to be many ideas competing for the lawmakers' time and attention. Often you must make appeals that will build a coalition of groups with varied and even competing agendas; you cannot afford to alienate too many members of your audience when you need a majority to support your proposal.

Do you think this passage is likely to convince the British Parliament that it should overturn a century-old law requiring a six-month quarantine of all animals entering the country?

> In effect, there is a vicious cycle in which the British government helps to inspire terror of rabies in the British public, and the public in turn demands that the government maintain the highest possible level of rabies protection, whatever the cost. It is difficult not to conclude that neither side has stopped to take a look at the facts and actually weigh all the pros and cons of the rabies law.

This simple paragraph manages first to remind members of the audience that the constituency they serve is strongly against the writer's proposal, and then to insult both the audience and the public by accusing them of acting (or not acting) without thinking. This approach is not likely to persuade the audience to change a long-standing, popular policy. Might this approach work better?

> The United Kingdom's law requiring a six-month quarantine of all pets that are brought into the country violates the plain meaning of the Treaty of Rome. The law is no longer necessary in light of the minimal threat that rabies poses to residents of medically advanced nations. The quarantine law is a financial and emotional burden on all European Union citizens who wish to bring pets into Britain, unnecessarily restricts the freedom of movement of pet-owning EU citizens, and results in the suffering of the thousands of animals per year who are confined in kennels during the quarantine process. Ladies and gentlemen of Parliament, I ask you to vote for the abolition of this unnecessary and anachronistic law.

This version offers fact-based arguments that undermine the stated logic behind the law and refrains from judging the audience for previously enacting or supporting the law. By also suggesting that circumstances have changed, it takes an approach that is much better designed to get the audience to take a fresh look at a century-old law.

Put yourself in Congress and think about whether you are likely to find this argument for health care reform persuasive.

> The current system is dominated by the powerful and rich insurance companies and health care providers which have fought so hard to maintain the status quo. This should surprise no one. These companies

have become fat charging exorbitant rates for their services, and often refusing to insure those with the greatest needs.

As has been readily apparent in the past weeks, change will not be easy. The powerful lobbies hired by the insurance companies have sent their minions to Capitol Hill to fan the flames of fear while spreading misinformation and lies about the plan.

Too many times I have seen that money can buy influence and votes in this body. However, I should remind you that with an issue such as this, which touches so many Americans, your vote on this bill will be scrutinized. Should you choose to serve the powerful interests desperate to maintain the status quo instead of your constituents, I promise you that you will be held accountable.

If you have worked with lobbyists in the past, are you likely to feel that your vote was purchased, or that you were simply persuaded to do the right thing? While an audience composed of members of the general public might react very well to these arguments, a substantial number of Congressional representatives might be annoyed or even offended by the implications of the argument. The writer is using scare tactics to persuade. Open contempt for the audience is far more likely to produce rationalization and retrenchment than change. Compare this argument:

But far too many Americans have been left out in the cold wondering what will happen to them or a loved one. For too many Americans who cannot afford insurance, poverty is only an aging parent in need of care or a sick child away. This is unacceptable and we can do better! Families fortunate enough to afford coverage often find, after years of paying premiums, that when they need insurance their benefits are capped by so-called lifetime insurance limits, which are used up long before their condition improves. This is unacceptable and we must do better. Other Americans suffering illnesses find that in their time of greatest need they are simply dropped and find it virtually impossible to find coverage elsewhere. The crisis is one of affordability and availability. As an example of how much health care costs have skyrocketed: In 1981 the average American family paid about $145 a month for health care while today that same family is likely to pay more than $430 a month for the same coverage. We can and must do something to reform this system.

This argument offers supporting facts and gives the legislators an idea of how their constituents are being hurt by the current system. Focusing on constituents rather than the legislators themselves appeals to the legislators' better instincts and reminds them why they are in office. Empirical data and the needs of constituents are much more useful persuasive tools for lawmakers than personal attacks and threats.

Arguments that are excessively dry and legalistic are equally unlikely to persuade lawmakers. Although lawmakers make the laws, they are not all trained in the law. For example, the following argument to a city council might work reasonably well in an appellate brief, but it is likely to lose the intended audience pretty quickly.

Obviously, an important factor is how Bill 10-8 would affect existing case law. The case which governs this issue is *Ibn-Tamas v. United States*. In 1979, the court of appeals reviewed a homicide case in which the trial court had excluded expert testimony about battered women. The court of appeals remanded the case, ruling that expert testimony about battered women can be admitted under current law, if the trial court found the expert had sufficient skill, knowledge, or experience in the field, and if the methodology used in the expert's study on battered women had been generally accepted by the scientific community. This ruling restates the second and third prongs of the *Dyas* test for the admissibility of expert testimony. On remand, the trial court concluded that the defendant failed to establish that the expert's methodology for studying battered women had been generally accepted by the expert's colleagues. The court of appeals upheld the trial court's finding on the ground that it was not clearly erroneous.

This decision goes against the trend today, which points toward admitting expert testimony on domestic abuse when it is possibly relevant. The increasing acceptance of domestic abuse testimony is partly due to the American Psychological Association's endorsement of its use beginning in 1984. Furthermore, in 1991, the United States Congress passed a resolution stating that "specialized knowledge of the nature and effect of domestic violence is sufficiently established to have gained general acceptance," and that expert testimony "concerning the nature and effect of domestic violence, including descriptions of the experience of battered women, should be admissible when offered in a state court."

The following approach is much clearer and more concrete, and more likely to give the lawmakers positive and comprehensible reasons to support the proposal:

Expert testimony helps explain to a trier of fact that a lay person's perceptions of what would be a "normal" or reasonable reaction to a batterer are different from the actual behavior and mentality of a battered woman. For example, experts can testify how battered women may reasonably believe that calling the police is futile because, even when called, the authorities frequently fail to respond to "domestic" incidents. Experts can explain that a battered woman's inability to leave her batterer may be due to social and economic reasons, such as that the victim's family does not accept a woman leaving a marriage or the victim simply cannot afford to leave because she and her children are financially dependent on the batterer. In addition, the expert can explain that the victim had a reasonable fear that her batterer would follow her if she left and inflict greater injury as punishment for leaving. Testimony that explains why it was reasonable for a battered woman to stay with her batterer helps to bolster the defendant-battered woman's credibility and helps to show that the woman's belief in the necessity of force was reasonable as well.

Expert testimony can also help to explain why resorting to deadly force against a weaponless assailant may have been reasonable. A battered woman may reasonably come to believe that her companion is capable of killing or seriously injuring without the use of a weapon. Very often, the woman will have experienced first-hand how near-death she could be, solely from her partner's weaponless hands and fists.

Any time you write to persuade audiences who have not been trained in the law, be especially sensitive to the need to use simple, concrete language and to explain technical concepts clearly. Put yourself in the audience's position and think about the expectations you would have and the arguments that would make you want to take the proposed action.Then do your best to meet those expectations and make those persuasive arguments.

EXERCISES

1. Your client is a landlord who wants to evict a tenant. The tenant has been paying only part of the rent, because the landlord has not made requested repairs. Also, the tenant is not the sort of upscale individual the landlord would like to attract to the building.

a. Please rewrite this letter to a client. Explain the concepts in terms a lay client could understand and omit any information the client is unlikely to need.

As a factual predicate, you indicated that you recently acquired an apartment complex. You are the sole proprietor and your intentions are to renovate the building into an upscale development that will attract higher income tenants—"yuppies." Your primary reason for seeking my advice, however, is that you anticipate difficulties with one of your tenants, Ms. Graves. As a legal introduction, let me interject that state law is embodied in the orders of the state legislature as well as in the decisions of the state courts. Therefore, some of the answers I will provide may stem from the state legislature—a statute, others may stem from court decisions—case law.

Fortunately, this state does not appear to require that a landlord pay the relocation costs of its tenants. A court decision that helps arrive at this conclusion is *Rockville Grovesnor, Inc. v. Montgomery County*. In 1980, in Montgomery County, the issue came up of whether a landlord was required to pay the relocation costs of tenants where an apartment building was undergoing conversion into condos. In that case, Montgomery County had a local ordinance that required that the landlord pay relocation costs. That ordinance was held invalid by the court. As a corollary of this decision, it would appear that a court would not require that you pay relocation costs to your present tenants in order for you to renovate your building. Nevertheless, more research is needed. Also, your willingness to allow Ms. Graves to credit the $300 that she owes toward the storage of her belongings during the renovation period is probably a prudent tactical decision.

In the event Ms. Graves institutes a rent escrow action and you decide to institute eviction proceedings against her, we must guard against having that action perceived as retaliatory. An eviction or arbitrary increase in rent solely because the tenant filed a suit against the landlord is prohibited unless it occurs six months after the determination of the initial court case. Thus, rather than an eviction proceeding, you may want to consider filing an action seeking to obtain only the rent itself. Such an action or suit is called "distress for rent." In general, if the lease contains no provision as to repairs, the landlord may not be bound to make repairs. Therefore, an action to obtain the rent instead of an eviction is not prohibited and will not be viewed as retaliatory. Obviously, facts pertaining to the lease and the provisions contained therein will be important.

b. Please rewrite the following paragraph so the client could retain you to represent him with some degree of confidence. This letter is to the same client as in the previous exercise; the tenant who had not been paying rent was also mugged on the grounds of the apartment building.

Assuming that all of the facts that I received from you are one hundred percent accurate, I think you are limited in terms of the options that are available to you at this time. Your situation with Ms. Graves is a very tricky one. A landlord has a duty to exercise reasonable care for tenants' safety by keeping common areas in a reasonably safe condition. When no duty exists, a landlord who voluntarily provides security measures can constitute a breach of duty. With respect to the mugging, you are willing to work something out with Ms. Graves to ease the transition period at Shady Nook. However, she has not yet made any efforts to take any action against you. It is possible that she does not intend to do so. If so, you will be taking steps to prevent a problem that you have yet to be faced with. It looks as though you might be liable for Ms. Graves' attack to a certain extent. My suggestion on this particular point would be to wait until Ms. Graves takes legal action against Shady Nook before attempting to reach an agreement with her about some type of compensation for the attack. If she does take legal action, we will address a settlement at that time.

2. Please rewrite this argument to Congress so that it is less likely to offend members of the audience. Suggest ways the writer could strengthen the appeal to give the legislators positive reasons to support the proposal.

Groups such as the National Rifleman's Society have successfully intimidated members of Congress from voting against laws as innocuous as preventing dangerous felons from buying handguns or preventing the sale of assault weapons. Business lobbies such as the Banking Lobby and the Insurance Lobby have spent their money to insure favorable treatment under the federal tax laws that keeps them exempt from taxation of certain transactions while other businesses are not. The list goes on and on. These are just a few examples of the abuses and inequitable outcomes of our current lobbying system. Those who have the most money to spend wield the most influence on those who make the laws. This bill would help prevent that. This bill will help ensure that House members will respond more to their constituents back in their districts, by limiting the power and the influence of the money-wielding lobbyists. After all, what is it that "representatives" are supposed to do? They are supposed to represent the people from their districts and the interests of those people from their districts, not the interests of the cash wielding political action committees who lurk in the shadows of the lobbies of Congress. This bill will curtail the "fourth" branch of the United States government: the lobbyists who intimidate our Congressional members by threats of supporting their opponents with big campaign bucks if they dare oppose them.

CHAPTER 8

WRITING FOR LEGAL AUDIENCES

When you write for audiences who have been trained in the law, primarily judges and lawyers, you still need to consider the particular needs of each audience. Although you can use more technical terminology and assume more familiarity with legal concepts, you must present your arguments in a way that makes each audience more receptive to adopting the course of action you advocate.

[1] Writing for Judges

Many lawyers frustrate judges by not adequately considering their needs and limitations. Judges are busy people who need lawyers to give them clear, succinct, well-supported, and well thought out reasons for deciding a case in a particular way. They need lawyers to ask for specific remedies and to justify the remedies in ways the judges can accept. Many of the chapters in this book offer ways to present arguments so they will be easier to comprehend, more interesting, and more persuasive. We do not intend to rehash that advice here. Instead, we focus on one specific aspect of thinking of judges as audiences: identifying the types of arguments and language most likely to persuade particular types of judges.

[a] Writing for Trial Judges

Whether you are writing a trial brief, or drafting opening statements or closing arguments to be delivered to a trial judge, consider the judge's function and what he or she needs to perform that function effectively. The trial judge's function is to evaluate the evidence, determine the facts, and then apply the law to the facts. Thus you must present the facts logically and efficiently and in a manner that leaves the judge with no choice but to conclude that governing law requires a judgment in your client's favor. You must also state the law succinctly and explain how the facts of the case fit into existing law. You must perform these tasks using appropriate language that is clear and concrete. It should also maintain a formal and respectful tone that acknowledges the significance of the occasion.

[i] Make Appropriate Arguments.

If you make presentations that are overly convoluted or that focus on facts or arguments that a trial judge is likely to consider irrelevant or unpersuasive, you will only frustrate the judge and increase the likelihood that the judge will find for your opponent. If you were a judge, trying to figure out exactly what happened, and what the law should do about it, how would you react to an opening statement containing this language?

> Good afternoon. May it please the court, my name is _____ and I represent the defendant in this case. The government alleges that my client engaged in a scheme to defraud the United States that lasted since the early 1970's. But there is one thing the government has overlooked—my client's 40 years of exemplary public service. The accusations raised against my client are simply incompatible with his distinguished and dedicated public service. In an era of "Congress-bashing" and in a time when the sentiment of "throw the old guy out" is preached with almost religious zeal and fervor, my client has become merely the latest victim of the anti-Congress vultures circling the Capitol's rotunda.
>
> In short, Your Honor, the prosecution will not be able to show beyond a reasonable doubt that my client is guilty of a scheme to defraud the government. The last thing my client would want to do is tarnish his reputation and his place in history—two things for which he has worked a lifetime. My client has faithfully served his constituents and his country for over 40 years; these charges and allegations are simply incompatible with his record. Accordingly, at the close of all the evidence, we will ask that your honor return the only possible verdict, a verdict of not guilty.

Is the judge likely to conclude that because the defendant has been in public service for many years, he could not have committed a crime? Or. that the prosecution should be dismissed because it may have some political consequences? It is barely possible that such arguments may have an impact on a jury; the judge, however, is much more likely to be persuaded by a presentation suggesting that the prosecution cannot prove all of the required elements of the crimes charged. Here is a defense presentation that is better designed to meet the judge's needs, because it focuses on the facts and identifies the key weakness in the prosecution's case.

> The stationery store is located in the Capitol building, and members of the legislature can purchase supplies as well as personal items. If the members purchase personal items, a set of rules details how the members are to pay for them. The defendant will tell the court about the procedural rules that govern the stationery store. He will admit that he mistakenly charged personal items to his official expense account. He will also tell the court that he has already made restitution for these items and any others about which there may have been any speculation at all. However, there will simply be no evidence of any intent to improperly purchase these items, as required by the criminal law. As a result, the government's evidence will be insufficient regarding the

stationery store, just as it will be insufficient for each situation the government must prove.

Consider this portion of a closing argument by the prosecutor in the same case.

> Your Honor, we are here today because a man in a powerful political position ripped off the citizens of the United States. This is about a man who was elected into political office on at least ten different occasions, to serve the people and to serve his country. A man who, once in office, found that he had a lot of power. Now, our Constitution gives power to the representatives of the American people so they can serve the public. Those representatives, whom we elect, have our trust. They hold the key to our security and our hopes. Your Honor, we are here today because the defendant abused that power. He violated our trust. But worse still, he lied to and cheated the American people.

This argument, both in language and focus, is again much better calculated to appeal to a jury than to a judge who is required to articulate a legal basis for his or conclusions. The language is somewhat condescending, and the argument seems designed to create a sense of personal betrayal. Is this good strategy for a prosecutor, who must prove every element of every crime charged beyond a reasonable doubt? Here is a better example of a prosecution closing argument.

> The government has demonstrated that the defendant, not his godson who mowed his lawn, not his cleaning or laundry servants, not his son-in-law, nor the engraver, but the defendant alone maintained detailed control over his payroll operations at all times. Only the defendant was responsible for submitting monthly payroll certification forms, detailing all the named employees, the dates they worked, and their duties. And only the defendant submitted these papers with his signature and no official duty entered on them. Therefore, Your Honor, the government has shown that the defendant knew that he was not supposed to pay these persons, but instead he charged their "salaries" to the government for their benefit or his own benefit in the form of cash kickbacks. These actions caused the government to pay more than $500,000 to so-called clerks of the defendant, by his concealment of material facts, embezzlement and conversion of public funds, and obstruction of justice. These are the facts, these are the actions of the defendant, and these are the crimes of the defendant.

This argument focuses on specific facts, and it connects those facts to the elements of the crimes with which the defendant has been charged. Such an approach meets the needs of the judge, because it gives him or her a basis for a ruling that is both within the law and consistent with the function of a trier of fact.

Here is one final example. If you were trying to convince a trial court not to allow a particular category of expert testimony at trial, how would you expect the judge to react to this argument in your trial brief?

> In *Smith* the Supreme Court of Columbia noted the inherent weakness of expert testimony regarding the Battered Woman Syndrome when used in support of a claim of self defense and declared such testimony "minimally relevant." Furthermore, as discussed above, even though such testimony may be "minimally relevant," it will almost always run afoul of Federal Rule of Evidence 403, and thus be deemed inadmissible. Federal Rule of Evidence 403, as are all the Rules of Evidence, is applied ad hoc, and in some cases a trial judge may not fully appreciate the amount of jury confusion that may result from the admission of such testimony. This situation gives rise to unpredictable determinations on the admissibility of such testimony. Accordingly, for the sake of judicial predictability, the Supreme Court of Columbia should adopt the position of several other jurisdictions and hold that expert testimony on the Battered Woman Syndrome is inadmissible.

Is the suggestion that the trial judge "may not fully appreciate the amount of jury confusion" likely to persuade the judge to rule in your favor? What is the trial court supposed to do with the suggestion that the state's highest court should change its previous ruling? You would demonstrate greater respect for the judge's ability to conduct a trial and be more likely to persuade the judge to rule in your favor if you made the argument this way:

> In *Smith* the Supreme Court of Columbia noted the inherent weakness of expert testimony regarding the Battered Woman Syndrome when used in support of a claim of self defense and declared such testimony "minimally relevant." Furthermore, as discussed above, even though such testimony may be "minimally relevant," it will almost always run afoul of Federal Rule of Evidence 403, and thus be deemed inadmissible. Because evidentiary rules are applied ad hoc in the particular circumstances of each trial, there is the possibility of unpredictable and inconsistent determinations on the admissibility of such testimony. Accordingly, to encourage judicial predictability, this court should hold that expert testimony on the Battered Woman Syndrome is inadmissible.

[ii] Use Appropriate Language.

When you write for a trial court, write in a clear, concrete, straightforward manner. Make your arguments simple and easy to understand, and make sure you present them in an appropriately formal and respectful tone. If you were a trial judge reading this statement of facts in a trial brief, how would you react? This excerpt is from a brief written on behalf of a battered spouse accused of trying to murder her husband.

Barbara Townsley asked her husband Nick to restrain his verbal outbursts, and then cautioned him of the high probability that the police would take him into custody if he failed to do so. Ignoring her advice, Nick loudly declared that he did not need instructions on how to live his life from someone whom he perceived to be a female dog. Nick then struck Barbara. This action prompted one of the members of the apartment community who had assembled to view the altercation to state his intention to notify the authorities.

. . .

Barbara defended herself with the frying pan, which she had inadvertently brought outside with her, because she was washing it at the moment Nick rushed out the door. In the course of defending herself, Barbara hit Nick once in the head with the frying pan. Not even fazed by the blow, Nick jerked the frying pan from Barbara and struck her with it. Only by scrambling away did Barbara avoid another painful encounter with the cooking utensil.

The tone of the writing is highly inappropriate—it is sarcastic and suggests that the lawyer is not taking the case seriously. If the lawyer cannot convey outrage and sympathy for his or her own client, how is the judge supposed to react? In addition to suggesting a lack of respect for the client, the somewhat flippant use of language suggests a similar lack of respect for the court. Although the writer may have been trying to be creative and make the story interesting, the judge is not likely to see it that way. Here is a more direct and persuasive way to present the same facts.

Barbara Townsley asked her husband Nick to stop yelling at her and then threatened to call the police if he did not stop. In response, Nick loudly declared that he did not need instructions on how to live his life from a "bitch." Nick then struck Barbara. This action prompted one of the neighbors to offer to call the police.

. . .

Barbara defended herself with the frying pan, which she had inadvertently brought outside with her because she was washing it at the moment Nick rushed out the door. In the course of defending herself, Barbara hit Nick once in the head with the frying pan. Not even fazed by the blow, Nick jerked the frying pan from Barbara and struck her with it. Only by scrambling away did Barbara avoid more serious injury.

Does the next portion of the same trial brief sound like advocacy or a law review article? Think about how you might rewrite the passage to make it more persuasive to the judge who must decide whether to admit the evidence.

The defendant in this case is pleading "not guilty" to all charges by asserting self-defense. In relying on self-defense, the defendant cites the traditional theories associated with the doctrine, as well as the more recent theory of Battered Woman Syndrome. It is the position of the defendant that traditional self-defense can be proven sufficiently to result in the defendant's acquittal. The defendant contends that self-defense, when supported by Battered Woman Syndrome, meets the acquittal standard of preponderance of the evidence.

The highest court of this state has held that evidence of Battered Woman Syndrome is admissible as minimally relevant. *Smith v. State.* The holding is in accord with decisions of a majority of the states, a majority that is increasing with time. As the cases discussed below will show, there are compelling reasons for affirming and even strengthening the Supreme Court's decision in *Smith.* According to American Jurisprudence, numerous courts hold that expert evidence of the Battered Woman Syndrome is admissible, but that some don't.

You need to focus much more directly on the role of the trial judge in this evidentiary dispute. You would rewrite the passage using more concrete language and explaining exactly what you intend to prove. Your rewrite might look something like this.

Barbara Townsley is pleading "not guilty" to all charges because she was defending herself from an attack by her husband. In relying on self-defense, Ms. Townsley urges the court to hear expert testimony regarding the Battered Woman Syndrome. This testimony will allow the jury to understand how the traditional elements of self defense apply here.

The highest court of this state has held that evidence of Battered Woman Syndrome is admissible. *Smith v. State.* This holding is in accord with decisions of a majority of the states, a majority that is increasing with time.

[b] Writing for Appellate Judges

Most of us began writing for appellate judges in our first year of law school. The typical introductory legal writing course ends with a moot court brief and appellate argument. How many of us really understood what it meant to be appearing in an appellate court? The phrase "standard of review" seemed like some arcane mantra that we were required to utter, but should not be required to comprehend.

There is no magic language that will persuade an appellate judge; writing clearly, concretely, and with appropriate formality will work in this context as well as it will in the trial context. Our focus in this section is on writing arguments that demonstrate an understanding of the role of the appellate judge. As with any other audience, if you write in a way that satisfies the appellate judge's expectations and gives the judge a reason to rule in your favor that is appropriate in the appellate context, you are much more likely to be persuasive.

The way to begin is to think about the function of an appellate judge. The judge must decide whether the judge or jury below made an error in applying the law. The appellate judge sees no evidence, hears no testimony, and can find no facts. On these matters, he or she must rely on the trial judge's evaluation. The appellate judge cannot begin to perform a legal assessment without knowing how much deference he or she is required to give the decision of the lower court. The issue of deference is why the concept of standard of review takes on such importance. The appellate judge is further constrained by other judicial rulings that might have precedential value. On the other hand, compared to the trial judge, the appellate judge has more freedom to consider social policies and trends in the law, at least where there is no clearly applicable binding precedent.

If you were an appellate judge, operating under these constraints, how would you react to this argument? The writer is arguing that the court should reverse the trial court's grant of summary judgment in favor of the appellees, a group of abortion protesters.

> Summary judgment was granted in favor of the appellees, Operation Cease and Desist, Terry Rand, Mary Rand, and Maria Leary. The court based its decision upon the premise that to bring an action under RICO, an economic motive is necessary. Appellant, The Pro-Choice Clinic, Inc., now urges this court to overturn summary judgment because an economic motive is not a requirement for invoking the provisions of RICO.

> . . .

> One of the main reasons the District Court granted summary judgment for Cease and Desist was because the court chose to follow the holdings of a few Second Circuit cases. Although it may seem that these cases require an economic motive, in reality, they contradict themselves or were later limited by the Supreme Court.

> As shown earlier, the economic motive as found in *United States v. Ivic* rests on questionable legal grounds. In the same year, the Second Circuit, in *United States v. Bagaric*, conceded that "[i]t is clear that § 1962 does not, by its terms, require proof of ultimate improper economic motive."

> The *Bagaric* court stated that "motive itself is not generally an element of a particular offense. When Congress has required proof of motive it has generally done so for behavior not deemed blameworthy absent the immoral motive, and not otherwise punishable." This

exception would not apply to the case at hand because here Cease & Desist admitted it illegally entered the Pro-Choice Clinic, which would be otherwise punishable and was eventually. The Court went on to say that "RICO demands no such inquiry . . . no additional scienter requirement is imposed by the statute. To carry out a deeper inquiry into long-term or ultimate motive would be to require adjudication of a factor traditionally deemed not exculpatory." The court in this case could not seem to make up its mind and therefore created an unsound decision. To follow a holding so inconsistent would be inappropriate.

How persuasive is an appellate court likely to find what can only be described as "whining" about the decisions of other courts? There is little real analysis in this argument—merely characterizations and expressions of frustration. Here is a way to approach the same argument with your audience's needs firmly in mind.

The District Court granted summary judgment in favor of the appellees, Operation Cease and Desist, Terry Rand, Mary Rand, and Maria Leary. The court based its decision upon the premise that bringing an action under RICO requires an economic motive. Appellant, The Pro-Choice Clinic, Inc., now urges this court to overturn summary judgment because an economic motive is not a requirement for invoking the provisions of RICO.

. . .

The District Court granted summary judgment for Cease and Desist in reliance on Second Circuit decisions. Although these cases may require an economic motive under some circumstances, they do not require such a finding in this case.

In *United States v. Bagaric*, The Second Circuit conceded that § 1962 does not expressly require proof of ultimate improper economic motive. The court stated that "motive itself is not generally an element of a particular offense. When Congress has required proof of motive it has generally done so for behavior not deemed blameworthy absent the immoral motive, and not otherwise punishable." This exception would not apply to the case at hand because here Cease & Desist admitted that its members illegally entered the Pro-Choice Clinic, which is an otherwise punishable act. The Court went on to say that "RICO demands no such inquiry... no additional scienter requirement is imposed by the statute. To carry out a deeper inquiry into long-term or ultimate motive would be to require adjudication of a factor traditionally deemed not exculpatory." Similarly, the District Court should not have required proof of an economic motive in this case and should not have granted summary judgment.

Recall the example in section [1][a] that argued the likelihood of jury confusion if expert testimony regarding Battered Woman Syndrome were allowed at trial. While that passage is not likely to persuade a trial judge and, in fact, risked irritating the judge, it is well-designed for an appellate court. It focuses on the likelihood of inconsistent results at the trial level and urges the court to rule in a way that would encourage consistency and efficiency throughout the system. Such an appeal acknowledges the ability of the appellate court to consider policy arguments and to rule in a way that has widespread precedential value. It is less effective at the trial level because a trial judge's rulings can affect only the case immediately before the court. Remembering such functional differences between the courts is one key way to enhance your persuasive powers.

[2] Writing for Other Lawyers

We write to persuade other lawyers in many situations: we try to persuade our colleagues and superiors to adopt particular courses of action; we want our superiors to think we are capable and give us good evaluations, not to mention raises; and we want opposing counsel to see a matter from our client's perspective and offer a good settlement or agree to a specific provision in a transactional document. To accomplish these goals, we must write in a manner that is best calculated to have the desired result; that is, we must consider the needs and expectations of the individual we want to persuade.

What are the needs and expectations of attorneys to whom we are likely to write? We should assume that they are busy, that they are familiar with basic legal concepts and terminology but not necessarily with the specific area of the law we are writing about, and that they appreciate writing that conveys respect and formality appropriate for a law office. These expectations should lead us to write in a manner that includes these three characteristics:

* Efficiency
* Clear explanations of the law and the facts
* Professional tone

Consider this memo to a supervising attorney. The memo is supposed to evaluate the strength of the client's case and offer advice on whether to take the case. The client was "stalked" by a would-be suitor who harassed her by using e-mail. Now the client would like to sue for intentional infliction of emotional distress.

The amalgamation of Mr. Partlow's conduct with the consequential impact on how Ms. Stalkey conducts her everyday affairs has, according to her, resulted in her being unable to sleep and sustaining significant emotional distress to the degree that she considered professional counseling. Does she have a sufficient cause of action? Let us first consider the elements of the tort of intentional infliction of emotional distress, most clearly enunciated in two cases, *Pavilon v. Kaferly*, and *Plocar v. Dunkin Donuts*.

Both *Pavilon* and *Plocar* characterize the three essential elements of, and subsequent threshold for, finding intentional infliction of emotional distress. While the facts in *Pavilon* proved sufficient for the court to find grounds for a tort of intentional infliction, the court was not so easily persuaded by the complaint put forth in *Plocar*. And since you have asked me to ascertain the probability of success of Ms. Stalkey's claim, I feel it best to do so using a case that has withstood the scrutiny of a rigid standard, not one that has been found wanting. Furthermore, while the crucial test set forth in *Pavilon* is similar to that set forth in *Plocar* with regard to the core of the standard itself, there are slight differences in that *Pavilon* calls for truly extreme and outrageous conduct, thereby making it a slightly more rigid test than *Plocar*. Because of these two factors and the fact that *Pavilon* is the more recent case, I will rely more heavily on its standard as its precedential nature would prove much more persuasive overall.

The language of this memo is convoluted and overblown. The writer seems to be lecturing the audience and takes a very long time to get to the point. Indeed, the two paragraphs say very little. The reader is likely to find this memo frustrating and annoying. Here is a way you might rewrite this portion of the memo to better meet the needs and expectations identified above. The language does little more than provide context for the analysis to follow, but at least this version does so succinctly.

Ms. Stalkey has been unable to sleep and is considering professional counseling. To determine whether she has a cause of action for intentional infliction of emotional distress, we must examine the governing cases, *Pavilon v. Kaferly* and *Plocar v. Dunkin Donuts*. The court in *Pavilon* found grounds for intentional infliction, but the court in *Plocar* did not. Because *Pavilon* is more recent and seems to apply a slightly higher standard to the defendant's conduct, this memo will focus on that case.

The next example offers too much in the way of personal editorializing and commentary. While the writer may believe everything in this paragraph, the lawyer trying to decide whether to take the case is looking for an analysis of facts and law, not suggestions on how the client can get her life in order!

Clearly, Ms. Stalkey is distressed by the conduct of Mr. Partlow. I would definitely recommend that she visit a therapist and file a court ordered injunction against Mr. Partlow to stop his activities. When one looks at the facts presented so far, however, I do not believe that we have a strong case against Mr. Partlow for the intentional infliction of emotional distress. Ms. Stalkey's case for proving severe emotional distress rests on the actions she took to protect herself, namely the rebuilding of her computer, replacement of the hard drive and the refusal to use any on-line computer services. While I admit these actions are clearly expensive, I believe the defense would argue that they were neurotic overreactions to Mr. Partlow's actions. All Ms. Stalkey really had to do was change her computer code! This is a simple and very inexpensive procedure that would have stopped Mr. Partlow's access, if in fact he had the access claimed.

If you were to attempt to rewrite this paragraph to meet the needs of the audience, you would probably cut almost all of it. You might preserve the underlying facts as context for a serious discussion of whether she has suffered severe emotional distress. Everything else can be eliminated.

As a final example, consider this excerpt from a letter to opposing counsel in the same case. The writer was trying to establish a basis for making a settlement demand.

We will argue to the court that it has a moral obligation to society to compensate for distress caused by stalkers. We are dealing with a person who has blatantly defied the warnings by the police and our client to commit actions that are causing distress and disruptions in Ms. Stalkey's life. He acknowledges that his own conduct could be construed as stalking, yet he continues with increased severity in his actions. We cannot allow individuals to suffer at the hands of others who knowingly cause distress in an extreme and outrageous manner under the pretense of professing love. Placing victims in fear to the point where it disrupts their personal lives is extortion.

The language of this letter is unprofessional and intemperate. It is not likely to encourage the recipient to pursue negotiations; rather, counsel will probably begin preparing for trial on the belief that settlement discussions will be antagonistic and ultimately useless. Here is one way you might rewrite to open the door to discussions while still articulating the basis for your client's claim.

If forced to trial, we will argue that the court has a moral obligation to society to compensate for distress caused by stalkers. Your client defied warnings by the police and our client and committed actions that are causing distress and disrupting Ms. Stalkey's life. Ms. Stalkey should not have been made to suffer because of your client's professions of love. Placing victims in fear to the point where it disrupts their personal lives is conduct that requires compensation.

In all communications with other lawyers, efficiency and professionalism will enhance your ability to persuade. Your superiors will be more likely to appreciate and adopt your recommendations, and your opponents will be more likely to work with you in a constructive and productive manner.

You may have noticed a common thread throughout these two chapters on writing for particular audiences. Clear, concrete language and well-supported, well-organized arguments will work well with virtually any audience. Beyond that, remember to think about the needs and expectations of your specific audience. Are you using language the audience will understand? Are you making arguments that fit the audience's function? Is the tone of your writing appropriate for the audience and occasion? If you can answer yes to all of these questions, you will find that your writing is much more likely to have the persuasive impact you desire.

EXERCISES

1. Please rewrite this section of a trial brief to increase the likelihood that it would persuade the trial judge to permit expert testimony on Battered Woman Syndrome. Assume that you represent the defendant battered spouse. Then rewrite it for an appellate court. Assume that you represent the same client, who was convicted after the trial court barred expert testimony on Battered Woman Syndrome.

In order to successfully assert a defense of self defense, Barbara Townsley must prove by a preponderance of the evidence that she believed she was in imminent danger of unlawful bodily harm and that the use of such force was necessary to avoid the danger. All jurisdictions require satisfaction of the requirements. Jurisdictions differ on whether retreat is required and whether the reasonableness of the defendant must be evaluated according to a subjective or objective standard.

When a battered woman asserts self-defense in a situation where attempted homicide occurrs in the midst of a violent battering incident, a claim of self-defense is not extraordinary. A good chance of success exists because elements of self-defense, specifically the imminence of danger and the reasonableness of the deadly force, can be met in a traditional fashion.

Although this case appears to meet the requirements of traditional self-defense, it is possible that the defense has concerns that Barbara Townsley's state of mind will be misunderstood by a jury. The jury may believe that Barbara Townsley had the opportunity to retreat or that she provoked the final series of events leading to the shooting, or both. The elements of self-defense would therefore not be met.

To accommodate the perspective of a battered woman who attempts to kill in self-defense, and to counter the element of retreat in self-defense, the Columbia courts should strengthen the holding in *Smith* and allow testimony on Battered Woman Syndrome. A battered woman does not believe that she can leave her abusive husband. It is critical to a proper and complete defense to show the jury that she feared immediate danger when an ordinary person might not.

2. Please rewrite this portion of a memo to meet the needs of an attorney who is trying to decide whether to take the case. Your client was stalked by e-mail and wants to sue for intentional infliction of emotional distress.

The first element requires that Partlow's behavior must be truly extreme and outrageous. John's behavior is analogous to the defendant's in *Pavilon* in that it was indecent and was an offensive and persistent sexual pursuit. However, it seems that absent any physical threats, abuse of a position of authority, and a knowledge that Susan is particularly susceptible to emotional distress, it will be difficult to characterize the harassment as so outrageous "as to go beyond all possible bounds of decency, and to be regarded as atrocious, and utterly intolerable in a civilized community," as the courts have in these cases. However, the absence of these specific circumstances would not automatically preclude the recognition that John's conduct is truly extreme and outrageous. The allegations remain that he has frightened her, warned her that he has devised many methods to harass her, and that he has disregarded Susan's orders and the police's orders that he cease contact with her. The court does not rule that the cited behavior is the minimum standard, but it would not be difficult to distinguish a series of annoyances, and threats to annoy, which Susan's case consists of, from the serious behavior cited above. I would also like to point out that nothing in Susan's allegations provides proof that it was indeed John who sent the e-mail messages after the police told him to leave Susan alone. I have to admit that I am unfamiliar with e-mail, but I would suggest that this question be addressed if a complaint is in fact filed.

Based upon my findings, I feel that we would have a good chance at convincing the court that Mr. Partlow's actions against Ms. Stalkey constitute the tort of intentional infliction of emotional distress. I believe that the three elements for this tort have been met, and while there is an argument to the contrary, the argument in support of Ms. Stalkey's claim is the stronger one. The key focus is on whether or not Mr. Partlow's conduct was outrageous and excessive. The issues of intent and causation are pretty straightforward. What one person considers to be outrageous conduct, another may not. However, I feel the court in this instance will agree for the reasons argued above that the conduct of Mr. Partlow was outrageous and excessive, thus supporting Ms. Stalkey's claim of intentional infliction of emotional distress. The court should not wait to compensate stalking victims until they are actually physically harmed, for example, battery, rape, or even murder. To do so would encourage individuals to take the law into their own hands and make sure that any impending physical harm would not result.

Ms. Stalkey definitely does not have a clear cut and dried claim for intentional infliction of emotional distress, but I feel that a successful claim can be made. All elements for the cause of action can be met sufficiently. We will have to focus on the disregard of police warnings to prove that the extreme and outrageous conduct is present but in a different context than previous holdings. In addition, it is vital that we argue a moral policy argument aimed at compensation for stalking victims such as Ms. Stalkey. Following this strategy, we can produce a cause of action which has a reasonable chance of being ruled in our favor by the court.

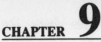

ADVOCACY AND ETHICS

You would like to delay a proceeding. May you do so by making an argument that you know lacks any merit? You do not want to tell the court that the material evidence you offered was false. May you justify nondisclosure by relying on lawyer-client confidentiality? You know of a case in your jurisdiction that is directly adverse to your client's argument, and your opponent has not cited it. May you choose not to bring it to the court's attention? The answer to these questions is no. Advocacy has its limits.

Ethical rules place constraints on zealous advocacy. As you know, all states impose ethical regulations on attorneys. In most states, the regulations track the American Bar Association's Model Rules of Professional Conduct. In other states, the regulations track the ABA's earlier effort, the Model Code of Professional Responsibility.

In this chapter, we set out the major ethical rules governing advocacy. Because most states follow the Model Rules, we focus the discussion on them. In the footnotes, we provide references to the Disciplinary Rules (DRs) of the Model Code. With respect to the material covered in this chapter, the Model Rules do not contradict the Model Code; instead, they often offer more detailed provisions.

In this short chapter, we explain what the rules require. Rather than offer a detailed analysis, we acquaint you with the most pertinent rules. In this way, we seek to prevent you from committing the most typical violations. If you encounter a situation that raises difficult ethical questions, we hope that this chapter will serve as a starting point for detailed research.[1]

We can summarize the most pertinent ethical precepts in four rules:

1. Make only meritorious claims, defenses, and arguments.

2. Do not make false statements to a tribunal or fail to disclose material facts.

3. Disclose adverse legal authority in the controlling jurisdiction.

4. In an ex parte proceeding, disclose all material facts.

---

[1] For detailed research, helpful sources include Monroe H. Freedman, Understanding Lawyers' Ethics (1990); Geoffrey C. Hazard, Jr. & W. William Hodes, The Law of Lawyering: A Handbook on the Model Rules of Professional Conduct (2d ed. 1990); Charles W. Wolfram, Modern Legal Ethics (1986).

[1] Make Only Meritorious Claims, Defenses, and Arguments

Model Rule 3.1 states:

> A lawyer shall not bring or defend a proceeding, or assert or controvert an issue therein, unless there is a basis for doing so that is not frivolous, which includes a good faith argument for an extension, modification or reversal of existing law. A lawyer for the defendant in a criminal proceeding, or the respondent in a proceeding that could result in incarceration, may nevertheless so defend the proceeding as to require that every element of the case be established.[2]

Although you must argue your client's case persuasively, you must not bring frivolous proceedings, raise frivolous defenses, or argue issues in a frivolous way. According to the Comment accompanying Model Rule 3.3:

> The action is frivolous if the client desires to have the action taken primarily for the purpose of harassing or maliciously injuring a person or if the lawyer is unable either to make a good faith argument on the merits of the action taken or to support the action taken by a good faith argument for an extension, modification or reversal of existing law.

The rule does not limit you to arguing settled law; you can make a good faith creative argument. Your argument is not frivolous if, in good faith, you seek to extend, modify, or reverse existing law. Moreover, your argument is not frivolous just because you believe that it will fail.

Rule 3.1 permits you as a criminal defense lawyer to require the government to prove all elements of its case without the defense's assistance. However, you still may not make frivolous arguments.

Here are two examples of frivolous arguments:

(1) A lawyer argues lack of jurisdiction by contending that the federal government can punish only those crimes committed in the District of Columbia and that the federal income tax is unconstitutional.[3]

---

[2] See Model Code of Professional Responsibility, DR 7-102(a); DR 2-109(A). Also worthy of attention is Rule 11 of the Federal Rules of Civil Procedure. When an attorney presents the court with a pleading, written motion, or other paper, Rule 11 requires the attorney to implicitly certify that to the best of the attorney's knowledge, information and belief, formed after a reasonable inquiry under the circumstances: (1) the paper is not being presented for an improper purpose; (2) the legal arguments are not frivolous; (3) the factual allegations have evidentiary support or are likely to after a reasonable opportunity for further investigation and study; and (4) the denials of factual contentions are warranted on the evidence or, if specifically so identified, are reasonably based on a lack of information or belief.

[3] See United States v. Collins, 920 F.2d 619, 623-24, 628 (10th Cir. 1990).

(2) Two doctors consult on a patient brought into the emergency room with a broken shoulder. The patient's lawyer brings an action against them for breaking the shoulder. After the lawyer learns the facts, he fails to drop the action.[4]

[2] Do Not Make False Statements to a Tribunal or Fail to Disclose Material Facts.

Model Rule provisions 3.3(a)(1)(2) & (4) state that a lawyer shall not knowingly:

(1) make a false statement of material fact or law to a tribunal;[5]

(2) fail to disclose a material fact to a tribunal when disclosure is necessary to avoid assisting a criminal or fraudulent act by the client;[6]

(4) offer evidence that the lawyer knows to be false. If a lawyer has offered material evidence and comes to know of its falsity, the lawyer shall take reasonable remedial measures.[7]

According to Rule 3.3(b), these duties continue until the proceeding concludes.[8] Complying may require disclosing information otherwise protected by Rule 1.6, which requires the attorney to keep confidential information relating to the representation of the client. Nonetheless, Rules 3.3(a) and (b) prevail.

Rule 3.3(c) states:

A lawyer may refuse to offer evidence that the lawyer believes is false.[9]

As these provisions make clear, when you communicate with a court or other tribunal, you must act with candor. You must not make material statements of law or fact that are false. When necessary to avoid assisting the client in a criminal or fraudulent act, you must disclose material facts.

---

[4] See Raine v. Drasin, 621 S.W.2d 895, 898, 900-901 (Ky. 1981).

[5] See DR 7-102(A)(5).

[6] See DR 7-102(a)(3).

[7] See DR 7-102(A)(4); 7-102(B)(2); 7-102(B)(1).

[8] The Model Code of Professional Responsibility has no comparable provision.

[9] The Model Code of Professional Responsibility has no comparable provision. If you encounter the problems of perjury and suspected perjury while representing a criminal defendant, you will not find consistent guidance on what you should do. According to most authorities, you first should urge your client to correct false evidence. If that effort fails, most authorities would provide two alternatives. First, if possible, withdraw your representation. Second, make a disclosure to the court. Likewise, most authorities would permit you to withhold evidence if you have reasonable doubts about its truthfulness. On this general topic, see 1 Hazard & Hodes, supra note 1, §§ 3.3:213 - 3.3:218.

In addition, you may refuse to offer information that you reasonably believe to be false.

When you make a statement that purports to be based on your own knowledge, for example, in an affidavit, you must make only statements that you know are true or are based on a reasonably diligent inquiry.

If you learn that you have offered material evidence that is false, you must take reasonable remedial measures. In most cases, you must disclose that the evidence was false.

If you do not know that evidence is false, but have reasonable doubts about its truthfulness, you have the discretion to introduce it or withhold it.[10]

Here are four examples of violations of the duty of candor:

1. An attorney receives notice of a deportation hearing from the United States Immigration and Naturalization Service. He fails to notify his client or to appear at the hearing. The INS orders the client deported. In an appeal, the attorney states that he never received notice of the hearing.[11]

2. In a social security proceeding, an attorney advises his client not to mention her second marriage and calls her by the name she used before her remarriage.[12]

3. In a divorce proceeding, the court awards custody of the child to the husband. In violation of a court order, the wife leaves the country with the child. Although the wife's attorney knows where the wife and child are, he refuses to disclose that information to the court.[13]

4. An attorney forges his client's signature on a document and then notarizes it, fraudulently representing that he witnessed the signing.[14]

[3] Disclose Adverse Legal Authority in the Controlling Jurisdiction

Model Rule 3.3(a)(3) states:

A lawyer shall not knowingly fail to disclose to the tribunal legal authority in the controlling jurisdiction known to the lawyer to be

---

[10] The Model Code of Professional Responsibility has no comparable provision.

[11] See Statewide Grievance Comm. v. Friedland, 609 A.2d 645, 648-49 (Conn. 1992).

[12] See In re Ver Dught, 825 S.W.2d 847, 850 (Mo. 1992).

[13] See Bersani v. Bersani, 565 A.2d 1368, 1370-72 (Conn. Super Ct. 1989).

[14] See In re Crapo, 542 N.E.2d 1334, 1334-35 (Ind. 1989).

directly adverse to the position of the client and not disclosed by opposing counsel.[15]

A close reading of the rule raises five points. First, you must disclose legal authority. Legal authority includes not just case law, but also statutes, regulations, ordinances, and administrative rulings.[16] If you fail to cite a pertinent adverse statute, for example, you can run afoul of the rule.

Second, you must disclose only adverse authority in the controlling jurisdiction. If you are litigating in a state trial court, you need to disclose adverse legal authority from state sources and from pertinent federal sources, for example, a decision by the United States Supreme Court. You need not disclose adverse cases decided in an adjoining state.

Third, you must disclose only authority directly adverse to your client's position. Even if the authority is not dispositive, it may be directly adverse and subject to the rule. For guidance in defining "directly adverse," Formal Opinion 280 (1949) of the American Bar Association Committee on Professional Ethics and Grievances is helpful.[17] It defines "directly adverse authority" as "directly adverse to any proposition of law on which the lawyer expressly relies, which would reasonably be considered important by the judge sitting on the case." The Committee offers this test:

> Is the decision which opposing counsel has overlooked one which the court should clearly consider in deciding the case? Would a reasonable judge properly feel that a lawyer who advanced, as law, a proposition adverse to the undisclosed decision, was lacking in candor and fairness to him? Might the judge consider himself misled by an implied representation that the lawyer knew of no adverse authority?

Fourth, you must disclose adverse authority only when opposing counsel fails to disclose it.

Fifth, you still may argue that the adverse authority does not control in your case—for example, your case is distinguishable from the adverse case on the facts. Alternatively, you may argue that it is bad law. Presumably you would make these arguments.

Even if we put aside the binding nature of the rule and the ethical duty to the tribunal, it makes practical sense not to hide important cases and other authorities. If the judge, the judge's clerk, or, belatedly, opposing counsel discovers the neglected adverse authority, you lose your credibility. As a result, you injure both your client and your reputation. Because your conduct may affect your success in future cases before the tribunal or against the same opposing counsel, you also injure your future clients.

---

[15] See DR 7-106(B)(1).

[16] See 1 Hazard & Hodes, supra note 1, § 3.3:206, at 587.

[17] For a reconfirmation of Formal Opinion 280, see ABA Comm. on Ethics and Professional Responsibility, Informal Op. 84-1505 (1984).

Here are three examples of violations of this rule:

1. In a brief to an intermediate appellate court, an attorney states that there are no cases on point and fails to note a case by the same court that the court finds to be dispositive of the issue before it.[18]

2. A city and a state tax commission are litigating a property tax issue. While the case is on appeal, the legislature enacts a statute that moots the issue. Neither attorney brings the statute to the court's attention.[19]

3. Litigation ensues when a manufacturer terminates a truck dealership. The manufacturer fails to cite a state statute requiring good cause to terminate a franchise agreement with a licensed new motor vehicle dealer. The manufacturer's attorney argues that he had no obligation to inform the court, because he believes that the statute is unconstitutional and that he has no obligation to suggest unpleaded claims or theories to the opposing side.[20]

[4] In an Ex Parte Proceeding, Disclose All Material Facts

Rule 3.3(d) states:

In an ex parte proceeding, a lawyer shall inform the tribunal of all material facts known to the lawyer which will enable the tribunal to make an informed decision, whether or not the facts are adverse.[21]

As the rule makes clear, in an ex parte proceeding—for example, an application for a temporary restraining order or a proceeding in which the opposing party defaults—you have an extensive duty of candor. Because no opposing attorney is present to make contrary arguments, your duty to the tribunal requires you to disclose more than the law and facts favorable to your client and more than the adverse legal authority required by Rule 3.3(a)(3).

As the Comment accompanying the rule states: "The lawyer for the represented party has the . . . duty to make disclosures of material facts known to the lawyer and that the lawyer reasonably believes are necessary to an informed decision."

Here are two examples of violations of the rule:

---

[18] See Thomas v. Workmen's Comp. Appeal Bd., 629 A.2d 251, 253 (Pa. Commw. Ct. 1993).

[19] See City of Okla. City v. Oklahoma Tax Comm'n, 789 P.2d 1287, 1297-1300 (Okla. 1990) (Opala, V.C.J., dissenting).

[20] See Dorso Trailer Sales, Inc. v. American Body Trailer, Inc., 464 N.W.2d 551, 554, 556-57 (Minn. Ct. App. 1990).

[21] The Model Code of Professional Responsibility has no comparable provision.

1. An attorney sues his client for $4,000 in unpaid attorney's fees. In obtaining a default judgment, he fails to disclose that the client had already paid him $2000 of that amount.[22]

2. Two attorneys representing separate plaintiffs win a favorable decision for a garnishment. The judge asks them to draw up a joint order for him to sign. While the process of jointly drafting the order goes on, one of the attorneys drafts an order providing recovery for only his client and submits it to a judge sitting in for the deciding judge. He fails to inform her of the material facts of the proceeding, notably the existence of another prevailing party.[23]

When it comes to legal ethics, there is some standard advice. Keep your nose clean. When faced with a choice, always take the high road. It is not bad advice.

---

[22] See Louisiana State Bar Ass'n v. White, 539 So. 2d 1216, 1220 (1989).

[23] See Fitzhugh v. Committee on Professional Conduct, 823 S.W.2d 896, 898-99 (Ark. 1992).

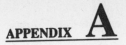
MAGIC WORDS: WRITING WITH FLAIR

Some writers can put words together in a way that allows us to see what they see, feel what they feel, and know what they know. Sometimes they have a talent for using metaphors and imagery—words that create just the right mental picture. Sometimes they choose words that make an argument sound so simple and so right that it becomes irrefutable.

Writing with flair does not mean overwriting. Overwriting includes exaggerating and making your argument with overblown rhetoric that merely distracts. The type of rhetorical flair we are discussing here does not have those characteristics. Instead, it uses images that are easy to understand and that make an argument clearer and stronger. It uses carefully chosen, simple words to make a compelling argument.

In this appendix, we offer some personal favorites as examples of the magic you can accomplish with the right combination of words. Although these examples were originally delivered in spoken formats, the rhetorical techniques apply equally to messages that are intended to be read silently rather than listened to.

The first collection of excerpts includes some exceptionally effective mental pictures. The second offers particularly persuasive advocacy that depends on using simple, concrete words to make a straightforward, compelling argument. When appropriate, we offer observations on the techniques used by the writers in the hope that identifying specific techniques may give you some tools to use in creating your own rhetorical magic.

METAPHORS AND IMAGERY

[1] METAPHORS

The following examples demonstrate each writer's ability to use metaphors, implicitly comparing essentially dissimilar things to create a concrete picture of an abstract idea. For example, if you say an idea "limps" or "stumbles," you are using a metaphor to create a mental image of a weak idea. When we can "see" or "feel" an idea, we are more likely to understand, retain, and perhaps adopt it as our own. We offer a selection of metaphors that ranges from well-developed, drawn out images to quick, sentence-long "vision bites."

ANDREW HAMILTON defends Peter Zenger against charges of libel, August 4, 1735

Power may justly be compared to a great river; while kept within its bounds, it is both beautiful and useful, but when it overflows its banks, it is then too impetuous to be stemmed; it bears down all before it, and brings destruction and desolation wherever it comes. If, then, this be the nature of power, let us at least do our duty, and like wise men who value freedom, use our utmost care to support liberty, the only bulwark against lawless power, which, in all ages, has sacrificed to its wild lust and boundless ambition the blood of the best men that ever lived.

WENDELL PHILLIPS protests the murder of abolitionist editor Elijah Lovejoy, Faneuil Hall, Boston, December 8, 1837

He [Lovejoy] took refuge under the banner of liberty—amid its folds; and when he fell, its glorious stars and stripes, the emblem of free institutions, around which cluster so many heart-stirring memories, were blotted out in the martyr's blood.

Public opinion, fast hastening on the downward course, must be arrested.. . . Haply, we may awake before we are borne over the precipice.

DANIEL WEBSTER speaks in the United States Senate, March 7, 1850

[H]e who sees these states, now revolving in harmony around a common center, and expects to see them quit their places and fly off without convulsion, may look the next hour to see the heavenly bodies rush from their spheres, and jostle against each other in the realms of space, without causing the wreck of the universe. There can be no such thing as a peaceable secession.

WENDELL PHILLIPS speaks before the Massachusetts Anti-Slavery Society at the Melodeon, Boston, Massachusetts, January 27, 1853

We are perfectly willing—I am for one—to be the dead lumber that shall make a path for these men into the light and love of the people.

HENRY THOREAU pleads for John Brown, 1859

The Republican party does not perceive how many his failure will make to vote more correctly than they would have them. They have counted the votes of Pennsylvania & Co., but they have not correctly counted Captain Brown's vote. He has taken the wind out of their sails,—the little wind they had,—and they may as well lie to and repair.

ELIZABETH CADY STANTON, 1872

I would have girls regard themselves not as adjectives but nouns
. . .

JOHN FITZGERALD KENNEDY delivers his Inaugural Address, January 20, 1961

And if a beachhead of cooperation may push back the jungle of suspicion, let both sides join in creating a new endeavor, not a new balance of power, but a new world of law, where the strong are just and the weak secure and the peace preserved.

REVEREND MARTIN LUTHER KING, JR. speaks at the LINCOLN MEMORIAL, August 28, 1963

But one hundred years later, the Negro still is not free. One hundred years later, the life of the Negro is still sadly crippled by the manacle of segregation and the chain of discrimination. One hundred years later, the Negro lives on a lonely island of poverty in the midst of a vast ocean of material prosperity. One hundred years later, the Negro is still languishing in the corner of American society and finds himself an exile in his own land. So we have come here today to dramatize a shameful condition.

In a sense we have come to the capital to cash a check. When the architects of our republic wrote the magnificent words of the Constitution and the Declaration of Independence, they were signing a promissory note to which every American was to fall heir. This note was a promise that all men—black men as well as white men—would be guaranteed the unalienable rights of life, liberty, and the pursuit of happiness.

But it is obvious today that America has defaulted on this promissory note insofar as her citizens of color are concerned. Instead of honoring this sacred obligation, America has given the Negro people a bad check—a check that has come back marked "insufficient funds." But we refuse to believe that the bank of justice is bankrupt. We refuse to believe that there are insufficient funds in the great vaults of opportunity in this Nation.

So we have come to cash this check. A check that will give us the riches of freedom and the security of justice.

. . .

I am not unmindful that some of you have come here out of great trials and tribulations. Some of you have come from narrow jail cells. Some of you have come from areas where your quest for freedom left you battered by the storms of persecution and staggered by the winds of police brutality. You have been the veterans of creative suffering. Continue to work with the faith that unearned suffering is redemptive.

. . .

I have a dream that one day on the red hills of Georgia the sons of slaves and the sons of former slaveowners will be able to sit down together at the table of brotherhood. I have a dream that one day even the state of Mississippi, sweltering with the heat of injustice, sweltering with the heat of oppression, will be transformed into an oasis of freedom and justice.

RICHARD MILHOUS NIXON delivers his Inaugural Address, January 20, 1969

The greatest honor history can bestow is the title of peacemaker. This honor now beckons America—the chance to help lead the world at last out of the valley of turmoil and on to that high ground of peace that man has dreamed of since the dawn of civilization.

PATRICK J. BUCHANAN speaks to the Daughters of the American Revolution, Constitution Hall, April 22, 1992

Like Gulliver, America is being tied down by the myriad tiny strands of this New World Order.

MARIO CUOMO nominates Bill Clinton at the Democratic Convention, July 15, 1992

Supply-side operated from the naive Republican assumption that if we fed the wealthiest Americans with huge income tax cuts, they would eventually produce loaves and fishes for everyone. Instead, it made a small group of our wealthiest Americans wealthier than ever, and left the rest of the country the crumbs from their table—unemployment, bankruptcies, economic stagnation.

And this time, this time we cannot afford to fail to deliver the message—not just to Democrats, but to the whole nation—because the ship of state is headed for the rocks. The crew knows it, the passengers know it; only the captain of the ship, President Bush, appears not to know it. He seems to think—no, no, no—you see, the President seems to think that the ship will be saved by imperceptible undercurrents directed by the invisible hand of some cyclical economic god that will gradually move the ship so that at the last moment it will miraculously glide past the rocks. Well, prayer is always a good idea, but our prayers must be accompanied by good works. We need a captain who understands that and who will seize the wheel before it's too late.

RONALD REAGAN addresses the Republican Convention, August 17, 1992

My dream is that you will travel the road ahead with liberty's lamp guiding your steps, and opportunity's arm steadying your way.

GEORGE BUSH addresses the Republican Convention, August 21, 1992

And you just won't hear that inflation, the thief of the middle class, has been locked in a maximum-security prison.

[2] OTHER IMAGES

These examples suggest the possibilities of using language in a way that creates concrete, sometimes humorous images, without technically employing the metaphor device. There is no implied comparison here, merely a use of words that allows us to visualize some aspect of the writer's message in a way that makes it clearer, more dramatic, and more interesting. Again, we offer a range of examples that demonstrates the use of imagery in everything from single sentences to several paragraphs. The type of image you create will depend on your audience, the context, and the point you are trying to make.

DANIEL WEBSTER addresses the Senate, January 26-7, 1830

That all may be so; but if the tribunal should not happen to be of that opinion, shall we swing for it? We are ready to die for our country, but it is rather an awkward business, this dying without touching the ground! After all, that is a sort of hemp tax worse than any part of the tariff.

WENDELL PHILLIPS protests the murder of abolitionist editor Elijah Lovejoy, Faneuil Hall, Boston, December 8, 1837

Sir, when I heard the gentleman lay down principles which place the murderers of Alton side by side with Otis and Hancock, with Quincy and Adams, I thought those pictured lips [pointing to the portraits in the hall] would have broken into voice to rebuke the recreant American—the slanderer of the dead. The gentleman said that he should sink into insignificance if he dared to gainsay the principles of these resolutions. Sir, for the sentiments he has uttered, on soil consecrated by the prayers of Puritans and the blood of patriots, the earth should have yawned and swallowed him up.

DANIEL WEBSTER addresses the United States Senate, March 7, 1850

And, now, Mr. President, instead of speaking of the possibility or utility of secession, instead of dwelling in those caverns of darkness, instead of groping with those ideas so full of all that is horrid and horrible, let us come out into the light of the day; let us enjoy the fresh air of Liberty and Union; let us cherish those hopes which belong to us; let us devote ourselves to those great objects that are fit for our consideration and our action; let us raise our conceptions to the magnitude and the importance of the duties that devolve upon us; let our comprehension be as broad as the country for which we act, our aspirations as high as its certain destiny; let us not be pygmies in a case that calls for men.

FREDERICK DOUGLASS speaks in Rochester, New York, July 4, 1852

To drag a man in fetters into the grand illuminated temple of liberty, and call upon him to join you in joyous anthems, were inhuman mockery and sacrilegious irony . . . .

Fellow citizens, above you national, tumultuous joy, I hear the mournful wail of millions! Whose chains, heavy and grievous yesterday, are, today, rendered more intolerable by the jubilee shouts that reach them.

WENDELL PHILLIPS addresses the Massachusetts Anti-Slavery Society at the Melodeon, Boston, Massachusetts, January 27, 1853

You load our names with infamy, and shout us down. But our words bide their time. We warn the living that we have terrible memories, and that their sins are never to be forgotten. We will gibbet the name of every apostate so black and high that his children's children shall blush to bear it. Yet we bear no malice—cherish no resentment. . . .

ELIZABETH CADY STANTON, 1872

These boys and girls are one today in school, at play, at home, never dreaming that one sex was foreordained to clutch the stars, the other but to kiss the dust . . . .

JOHN FITZGERALD KENNEDY delivers his Inaugural Address, January 20, 1961

The world is very different now. For man holds in his mortal hands the power to abolish all forms of human poverty and all forms of human life.

MARIO CUOMO addresses the Democratic Convention, July 17, 1984

The difference between Democrats and Republicans has always been measured in courage and confidence. The Republicans believe that the wagon train will not make it to the frontier unless some of the old, some of the young, some of the weak are left behind by the side of the trail.

The strong, the strong, they tell us, will inherit the land!

We Democrats believe in something else. We Democrats believe that we can make it all the way with the whole family intact.

And we have more than once.

Ever since Franklin Roosevelt lifted himself from his wheelchair to lift this nation from its knees. Wagon train after wagon train. To new frontiers of education, housing, peace. The whole family aboard. Constantly reaching out to extend and enlarge that family. Lifting them up into the wagon on the way. Blacks and Hispanics and people of every ethnic group and Native Americans—all those struggling to build their families and claim some small share of America.

. . .

To succeed we will have to surrender some small parts of our individual interests, to build a platform we can all stand on, at once, and comfortably, proudly singing out. We need a platform we can all agree to, so that we can sing out the truth for the nation to hear, in chorus, its logic so clear and commanding that no slick Madison Avenue commercial, no amount of geniality, no martial music will be able to muffle the sound of the truth.

. . .

It is a mortgage on our children's future that can only be paid in pain and that could bring this nation to its knees.

BILL CLINTON addresses the Democratic Convention, July 17, 1992

An America in which the rich are not soaked—but the middle class is not drowned, either.

RONALD REAGAN addresses the Republican Convention, August 17, 1992

Until then, when we see all that rhetorical smoke billowing out from the Democrats, well, ladies and gentlemen, I'd follow the example of their nominee—don't inhale.

GEORGE BUSH addresses the Republican Convention, August 21, 1992

Now, the Soviet bear may be gone, but there are still wolves in the woods.

. . .

It is a body caught in a hopelessly tangled web of PACs, perks, privileges, partisanship and paralysis. Every day, every day, Congress puts politics ahead of principle and above progress. [This last example demonstrates the use of alliteration—the repetition of initial sounds for dramatic effect.]

SIMPLE APPEALS

Sometimes the purity and simplicity of an argument are such that we cannot help but be persuaded. If the writer can identify objective principles with which the reader must almost certainly agree and attach those principles to the idea the writer is trying to convey, the reader is likely to be swept along to the writer's intended conclusion almost without realizing it. If the writer can also employ simple, concrete, perhaps even eloquent language that makes the idea easy to understand and believe in, the likelihood of persuasion becomes even greater. Here are some examples:

RED JACKET responds to a missionary at a council of chiefs of the Six Nations, 1805

Brother, you say there is but one way to worship and serve the Great Spirit. If there is but one religion, why do you white people differ so much about it? Why not all agreed, as you can all read the book?

. . .

Brother, we are told that you have been preaching to the white people in this place. These people are our neighbors. We are acquainted with them. We will wait a little while and see what effect your preaching has upon them. If we find it does them good, makes them honest, and less disposed to cheat Indians, we will then consider again of what you have said.

FREDERICK DOUGLASS speaks in Rochester, New York, July 4, 1852

It is admitted in the fact that Southern statute books are covered with enactments forbidding, under severe fines and penalties, the teaching of the slave to read or to write. When you can point to any such laws in reference to the beasts of the field, then I may consent to argue the manhood of the slave. When the dogs in your streets, when the fowls of the air, when the cattle on your hills, when the fish of the sea and the reptiles that crawl shall be unable to distinguish the slave from a brute, then will I argue with you that the slave is a man!

. . .

What, am I to argue that it is wrong to make men brutes, to rob them of their liberty, to work them without wages, to keep them ignorant of their relations to their fellow men, to beat them with sticks, to flay their flesh with the lash, to load their limbs with irons, to hunt them with dogs, to sell them at auction, to sunder their families, to knock out their teeth, to burn their flesh, to starve them into obedience and submission to their masters? Must I argue that a system thus marked with blood, and stained with pollution, is wrong?

ELIZABETH CADY STANTON, 1892

When there is a demand for healthy, happy, vigorous, self-reliant women, they will make their appearance. But with our feeble type of manhood the present supply of vanity and vacuity meets their wants. Woman, as she is today, is men's handiwork. With iron shoes, steel-ribbed corsets, hoops, trains, high heels, chignons, panders, limping gait, feeble muscles, with her cultivated fears of everything seen and unseen, of snakes, spiders, mice and millers, cows, caterpillars, dogs and drunken men, firecrackers and cannon, thunder and lightning, ghosts and gentlemen, women die ten thousand deaths, when if educated to be brave and self-dependent, they would die but one.

ELIZABETH CADY STANTON keynotes the first Woman's Rights Convention in Seneca Falls, New York, July 19, 1848

The right is ours. The question now is: how shall we get possession of what rightfully belongs to us? We should not feel so sorely grieved if no man who had not attained the full stature of a Webster, Clay, Van Buren, or Gerrit Smith could claim the right of the elective franchise. But to have drunkards, idiots, horse-racing, rum-selling rowdies, ignorant foreigners, and silly boys fully recognized, while we ourselves are thrust out from all the rights that belong to citizens, it is too grossly insulting to the dignity of woman to be longer quietly submitted to. The right is ours. Have it, we must. Use it, we will. The pens, the tongues, the fortunes, the indomitable wills of many women are already pledged to secure this right. The great truth that no just government can be formed without the consent of the governed we shall echo and re-echo in the ears of the unjust judge, until by continual coming we shall weary him.

. . .

The world has never yet seen a truly great and virtuous nation, because in the degradation of woman the very fountains of life are poisoned at their source. It is vain to look for silver and gold from mines of copper and lead. It is the wise mother that has the wise son. So long as your women are slaves you may throw your colleges and churches to the winds. You can't have scholars and saints so long as your mothers are ground to powder between the upper and nether millstone of tyranny and lust. How seldom, now, is a father's pride gratified, his fond hopes realized, in the budding genius of his son! The wife is degraded, made the mere creature of caprice, and the ·foolish son is heaviness to his heart. Truly are the sins of the fathers visited upon the children to the third and fourth generation. God, in His wisdom, has so linked the whole human family together that any violence done at one end of the chain is felt throughout its length, and here, too, is the law of restoration, as in woman all have fallen, so in her elevation shall the race be recreated.

WILLIAM JENNINGS BRYAN addresses the Democratic National Convention, July 8, 1896

You come to us and tell us that the great cities are in favor of the gold standard; we reply that the great cities rest upon our broad and fertile prairies. Burn down your cities and leave our farms, and your cities will spring up again as if by magic; but destroy our farms and the grass will grow in the streets of every city in the country.

CLARENCE DARROW makes his closing argument in the Leopold and Loeb case, Chicago, 1924

Your Honor stands between the past and the future. You may hang these boys; you may hang them by the neck until they are dead. But in doing it you will turn your face toward the past. In doing it you are making it harder for every other boy who in ignorance and darkness must grope his way through the mazes which only childhood knows. In doing it you will make it harder for unborn children. You may save them and make it easier for every child that sometime may stand where these boys stand. You will make it easier for every human being with an aspiration and a vision and a hope and a fate. I am pleading for the future; I am pleading for a time when hatred and cruelty will not control the hearts of men. When we can learn by reason and judgement and understanding and faith that all life is worth saving, and that mercy is the highest attribute of man.

CLARENCE DARROW makes his closing argument in the Henry Sweet trial, May 19, 1926

Let us take a little glance at the history of the Negro race. It only needs a minute. It seems to me that the story would melt hearts of stone. I was born in America. I could have left it if I had wanted to go away. Some other men, reading about this land of freedom that we brag about on the Fourth of July, came voluntarily to America. These men, the defendants, are here because they could not help it. Their ancestors were captured in the jungles and on the plains of Africa, captured as you capture wild beasts, torn from their homes and their kindred, loaded into slave ships, packed like sardines in a box, half of them dying on the ocean passage; some jumping into the sea in their frenzy, when they had a chance to choose death in place of slavery. They were captured and brought here. They could not help it. They were bought and sold as slaves, to work without pay, because they were black. They were subject to all of this for generations, until finally they were given their liberty, so far as the law goes—and that is only a little way, because, after all, every human being's life in this world is inevitably mixed with every other life and, no matter what laws we pass, no matter what precautions we take, unless the people we meet are kindly and decent and human and liberty-loving, then there is no liberty. Freedom comes from human beings, rather than from laws and institutions.

. . .

I do not believe in the law of hate. I may not be true to my ideals always, but I believe in the law of love, and I believe you can do nothing with hatred. I would like to see a time when man loves his fellow man and forgets his color or his creed. We will never be civilized until that time comes. I know the Negro race has a long road to go. I believe that the life of the Negro race has been a life of tragedy, of injustice, of oppression. The law has made him equal, but man has not. And, after all, the last analysis is: what has man done?—and not what has the law done? I know there is a long road ahead of him before he can take the place which I believe he should take. I know that before him there is sorrow, tribulation and death among the blacks, and perhaps the whites. I am sorry. I would do what I could to avert it. I would advise patience; I would advise tolerance; I would advise understanding; I would advise all those things which are necessary for men who live together.

RONALD REAGAN addresses the Republican Convention, August 17, 1992

In America our origins matter less than our destinations, and that's what democracy is all about.

MARY FISHER addresses the Republican National Convention, August 23, 1992

Tonight, I represent an AIDS community whose members have been reluctantly drafted from every segment of American society. Though I am white, and a mother, I am one with a black infant struggling with tubes in a Philadelphia hospital. Though I am female, and contracted this disease in marriage, and enjoy the warm support of my family, I am one with the lonely gay man sheltering a flickering candle from the cold wind of his family's rejection.

. . .

Tonight, HIV marches resolutely toward AIDS in more than a million American homes, littering its pathway with the bodies of the young. Young men, young women, young parents, young children. One of the families is mine. If it is true that HIV inevitably turns to AIDS, then my children will inevitably turn to orphans.

. . .

I want my children to know that their mother was not a victim. She was a messenger. I do not want them to think, as I once did, that courage is the absence of fear; I want them to know that courage is the strength to act wisely when most we are afraid. I want them to have the courage to step forward when called by their nation, or their party, and give leadership—no matter what the personal cost. I ask no more of you than I ask of myself, or of my children.

To my children, I make this pledge: I will not give in, Zachary, because I draw my courage from you. Your silly giggle gives me hope. Your gentle prayers give me strength. And you, my child, give me reason to say to America, "You are at risk". And I will not rest, Max, until I have done all I can to make your world safe. I will seek a place where intimacy is not the prelude to suffering.

I will not hurry to leave you, my children. But when I go, I pray that you will not suffer shame on my account. To all within the sound of my voice, I appeal: Learn with me the lessons of history and of grace, so my children will not be afraid to say the word AIDS when I am gone. Then their children, and yours may not need to whisper it at all. God bless the children, and God bless us all. Good night.

APPENDIX B

REVIEW EXERCISE

Here is an exercise that is designed to give you an opportunity to integrate many of the lessons we have discussed in this book.

Harvey Dunker, a long-time client, came into your office last week with a very sad story. On June 10, 1992, his wife Gertrude, a 43-year-old accountant from Virginia, gave birth to her first child, Danny. The delivering doctors pronounced Danny a victim of anencephaly, a rare birth defect that inhibits proper brain formation in unborn children. In Danny's case, he had only a poorly formed brain stem, which, along with intravenous feeding, would allow his autonomous systems to operate until his brain stem and other organs deteriorated to the point where they could no longer function. Doctors estimated this period would be no longer than three weeks.

During the first trimester of Ms. Dunker's pregnancy, Dr. Gillian Derais, the attending obstetrician, predicted the possibility of great health risks to both mother and child. Dr. Derais suggested terminating the pregnancy for three reasons: (1) a history of birth defects in Ms. Dunker's family; (2) her medical history of allergies, susceptibility to illness and infection, and generally poor immune system; and (3) her age.

The Dunkers discussed this option, but decided that they recognized their fetus as a human being. Ms. Dunker informed Dr. Derais of her intent to carry the baby to term and her reason for this decision.

As expected, the pregnancy was difficult, and the baby underwent a Caesarian delivery. During the procedure, Ms. Dunker suffered an allergic reaction to an anesthetic. As a result of these physical traumas, doctors required Ms. Dunker to remain hospitalized for at least two weeks.

No evidence exists linking Danny's anencephaly to the three factors cited by Dr. Derais.

On the day after the delivery, Mr. Dunker waited by his wife's bedside in the intensive care ward. A nurse delivered to them a letter written by Dr. Derais, which contained this paragraph:

> I share your grief in this sad hour. However, I must point out an opportunity to transform your loss into hope for other stricken children. While Danny lies lifeless, his slowly deteriorating organs could be harvested and transplanted into more viable children. His liver, pancreas, heart, kidneys, and even his corneas (if they don't prove too small) can be removed for placement into a home imbued

with life in order to restore the vigor that your child did not have. I urge you to complete the accompanying consent form and help save other unfortunate children.

The nurse informed the Dunkers that Dr. Derais could not personally deliver this message because she had to leave for an OB/GYN conference on Maui. He also mentioned that hospital regulations required that there be a written record of all requests for organ donations and consents to permit them. At that moment, Dr. Derais, wearing a Hawaiian print dress and carrying a suitcase and tennis racket, walked by the room and into a waiting elevator.

The Dunkers decided that it was immoral not to allow the death of their child to benefit others in need. They reluctantly signed the consent form.

The Dunkers have since learned that Danny was legally alive at the time his organs were harvested and transplanted into waiting recipients. While they recognize that he did not have any chance for a meaningful life, the Dunkers morally oppose the intentional termination of any life. Although they do not regret that Danny was able to provide life for other children, they are very unhappy with the way Dr. Derais handled the situation.

Ms. Dunker has had nightmares almost every night since the incident. In some of them, Danny rebukes her for letting the doctors "carve him up" almost as soon as he was born. In others, she sees Dr. Derais holding up Danny's little body parts and cackling maniacally. Needless to say, these dreams have caused her no small degree of distress and have disturbed Mr. Dunker as well. They feel that their lives have been completely disrupted by these events and that it will be a long time before they are able to reclaim any semblance of emotional stability. Mr. Dunker told you that he feels the transition was made much more difficult by Dr. Derais' callous behavior, and he wondered if they had any legal recourse.

You think these facts might support a claim for intentional infliction of emotional distress. These are the leading cases in your jurisdiction:

Sere v. Group Hospitalization, Inc.

> The elements of intentional infliction of emotional distress are: 1) extreme and outrageous conduct on the part of the defendant, that 2) intentionally or recklessly 3) causes the plaintiff severe emotional distress. It is possible to infer intent or recklessness from the outrageousness of the behavior. The emotional upset must be so acute that harmful physical consequences may result.

Anderson v. Prease

> Although an actor's conduct may not be considered extreme or outrageous in most circumstances, it may be characterized as such when the actor knows that the other person is peculiarly susceptible

to emotional distress. In *Anderson*, a doctor verbally berated a distraught patient he had been treating. The court found that the doctor's special knowledge of the patient's emotional state supported a finding of intentional infliction of emotional distress.

You give these facts and the applicable law to an associate and request two memos: one outlining the best arguments supporting the Dunkers' case, and the other outlining the best arguments for the opposition. This is the result:

Memo in Support of the Dunkers' Claim

First, Dr. Derais' behavior was both extreme and outrageous. Knowing that the Dunkers opposed the termination of any life, she still described Danny as "lifeless" and urged them to consent to organ removal. In the eyes of most people, urging parental consent for the removal of organs from an infant who is still legally alive, without informing the parents that the infant was legally alive, would seem extreme and outrageous.

Furthermore, according to *Anderson v. Prease*, "although the actor's conduct may generally not be considered extreme or outrageous, it may be characterized as such when the actor knows that the other person is peculiarly susceptible to emotional distress." Dr. Derais was aware of the Dunkers' moral opposition to intentional termination of life and should thus have been aware of the distress they would feel. Dr. Derais' conduct should not be modeled by other doctors. The doctor did not meet personally with the couple to discuss the situation. Instead she had a nurse deliver a letter urging the couple to allow the hospital to "harvest & transplant" their baby's organs. The letter was ambiguous in that it said the baby was lifeless.

Dr. Derais will probably argue that her insensitivity is not analogous to the abusive behavior in *Anderson*. This is not important. The letter is the main concern. It states, "While Danny lies lifeless, his slowly deteriorating organs could be harvested . . ." However, the letter never explicitly states whether the baby is dead or alive. Knowing that the Dunkers refused an abortion because they regarded the fetus as a human being, Dr. Derais should have inferred their moral objection to the intentional termination of life. Her omission of the baby's legal condition and her failure to make herself available to answer any questions concerning this subject, especially in light of the urgency the letter suggests, may meet the standard of outrageous conduct.

Second, Dr. Derais' conduct was intentional or reckless. Dr. Derais most likely did not intend to cause distress to the Dunkers; however, arguably, her behavior was reckless. She did not personally discuss the factors and consequences of the decision with the Dunkers, although she was in the hospital at the time the letter was delivered. Although she may have had a plane to catch, her attire suggests a vacation more than a professional obligation. Dr. Derais should have been aware that her use of the word "lifeless" in the letter would mislead the Dunkers into believing the infant was deceased. Knowing how they felt about intentional termination of life, Dr. Derais should have been more direct with the words used and more sensitive in handling the situation personally.

Third, Ms. Dunker continues to suffer "emotional upset of so acute a nature that harmful physical consequences might be not unlikely to occur." She has suffered severe emotional distress in the form of recurrent nightmares. These nightmares undoubtedly cause insomnia, which would limit Ms. Dunker's ability to function in daily activities. Insomnia in itself causes physical exhaustion and an overall weakening of her physical condition. There is no doubt that substantial loss of sleep is likely to have a range of harmful physical consequences. These nightmares have caused a great deal of distress to Mr. Dunker as well.

Memo in Opposition to the Dunkers' Claim

Although Dr. Derais knew that the couple opposed the aborting of their fetus, she did not necessarily know that the couple would be susceptible to emotional problems. The doctor knew of Ms. Dunker's physical problems, but not of any emotional problems. Thus, Dr. Derais' conduct would not be found to be outrageous under the prior knowledge definition. Although the doctor knew Ms. Dunker recently lost a child and was weak from the delivery, Dr. Derais was encouraging and compassionate in the letter. Dr. Derais had seen patients in this condition before, so she had no reason to know the Dunkers were more susceptible than others. There is no other proof that Dr. Derais had any knowledge of Ms. Dunker's susceptibility to emotional distress. Dr. Derais' only contact with the Dunkers is the consultation regarding terminating the pregnancy. Therefore, because Dr. Derais had no prior knowledge that the Dunkers were susceptible to emotional distress, it is unlikely her conduct can be considered extreme and outrageous.

The *Sere* case takes the issue of outrageousness one step further by stating that the conduct must be "so outrageous in character, and so extreme in degree, as to go beyond all possible bounds of decency, and to be regarded as . . . utterly intolerable in a civilized community." The only part of this claim the court may find outrageous is the fact that Danny was still legally alive at the time his organs were removed and the doctor did not personally inform the Dunkers that would be the case. However, doctors are extremely busy people with other patients to attend. In addition, the fact that the Dunkers saw Dr. Derais leaving for a convention is not beyond all "bounds of decency." Dr. Derais is a professional and professionals often go to conventions with colleagues, where they discuss new advances in medical technology.

In addition to outrageous conduct, intentional infliction of emotional distress requires that the actor be either acting intentionally or recklessly. The required intent of an act can be inferred from the outrageousness of the act. Because it is unlikely that Dr. Derais' act was outrageous, there is less of a possibility of inferred intent based on these facts.

Dr. Derais did not seem to intend to do any harm to the Dunkers, nor does it seem likely that the doctor's actions could be construed as reckless because she showed her sensitivity through the encouraging and compassionate letter, and helped the Dunkers transform their loss into a moral act of donation. It may be argued that the doctor knew the Dunkers do not support intentional termination of a life, but they signed a consent form for the harvesting procedure. In addition, Dr. Derais informed the Dunkers of all the potential harms of the pregnancy, let the Dunkers make all of their own informed decisions, and did not act except with the permission of the Dunkers. Dr. Derais has expressly shown her sensitivity by informing the Dunkers each step of the way and helping them turn a tragic situation into hope for others. Therefore, it is unlikely that Dr. Derais' actions could be considered intentional or reckless.

It is unlikely that the doctor's actions caused the Dunkers "severe emotional distress." In *Sere*, the court held that "the defendants' actions must proximately cause the plaintiff's emotional upset of so acute a nature that harmful physical consequences might be not unlikely to result." There is no doubt that Ms. Dunker is suffering from severe emotional distress; however, the issue is whether the doctor's actions caused the distress. Ms. Dunker has had terrible nightmares since she learned that her baby was legally alive at the time his organs were "harvested," but would she have had these nightmares regardless of the doctor's conduct? In this instance, the doctor's conduct might have contributed to the specific details of the dreams, but Dr. Derais' actions may not have precipitated the nightmares. With or without Dr. Derais' conduct, Ms. Dunker might have had nightmares.

The loss of a child, for whatever reason, is a hard ordeal to accept. There is no saying that even if the Dunkers had decided not to terminate Danny's life, Ms. Dunker might be having nightmares if Danny had died naturally. It is not sufficiently clear that the removal of Danny's organs is causing these nightmares. The nightmares could be caused by the fact that the Dunkers lost their only child and their probability of trying for another child is quite low, given Ms. Dunker's age.

Also, it is unclear whether nightmares are "harmful physical consequences." There is to this point no precedent that offers an opinion on whether nightmares may be considered a physical consequence. One may argue that insomnia and loss of sleep are physical consequences, but dreams alone are unlikely to be held by a court to be physical. Without such physical consequences, the third element of this tort will not be satisfied.

What suggestions would you give the associate? How would you rewrite the memos to make them clear and persuasive? Begin with this checklist, based on the lessons in this book:

_____ Is the information presented in an order that is easy to follow?

_____ Is the organization readily apparent?

_____ Are topic sentences used appropriately?

_____ Is the writing style concrete?

_____ Are words or ideas intended to be emphasized placed at the ends of sentences?

_____ Are sentence subjects used appropriately?

_____ Are equity and policy arguments integrated effectively?

_____ Is the audience adaptation appropriate?[1]

---

[1] This checklist is not an exhaustive summary of the lessons in the book. It is intended to focus your attention on some of the specific lessons the writer might have employed to better effect. You might want to consider designing your own checklist, incorporating lessons you found particularly instructive or that are most likely to improve your advocacy writing.